# HOW BECOME A VIRTUAL ASSISTANT

## START YOUR OWN
## BUSINESS FROM HOME

LAURA BRIGGS

Other Books by the Author


*How to Start Your Own Freelance Writing Business,*
Entrepreneur Press
*Six Figure Freelancer,* Entrepreneur Press

# PREFACE

Today, there are a lot of online courses out there aimed at aspiring virtual assistants. As a beginner myself years ago, I could never have afforded them when was just breaking in, and I'm guessing you can't, either. But I'm also guessing that you're willing to place a bet on yourself to do the hard work. I did starting back in 2012 and grew my freelance side hustle into a multi six-figure business. It all started with a few contracts. This book is designed to help you get started without needing to invest hundreds of dollars in an online course. But this book only works if *you* do.

Whether you're hoping for some extra cash on a part-time basis or have a goal of truly creating a full time income, the opportunities are up to you with virtual assisting. In this book, you'll get my best tips and recommendations on getting started after working with hundreds of students who broke into VA work.

Thanks to everyone on my advanced reader team, editor Felicity Fox, my own team of virtual assistants (shoutouts to Andrew & Melissa- you rock), and, of course, my husband John for helping this book come to life.

# CONTENTS

# INTRODUCTION: WHY NOW IS THE RIGHT TIME TO BECOME A VA

No man is an island. And no other person or business is either. Now more than ever, people realize that it's simply impossible to break past a certain point when running a business without outsourcing and hiring help. When this happens, the first hire is usually a virtual assistant. In 2019, there were over 57 million freelancers in the U.S., and a good portion of them worked online. Supply and demand are rising for virtual assistants, which is probably a big part of the reason you bought or downloaded this book.

I started working online as a virtual assistant (VA) in 2012 and have hired, trained, or worked with over five dozen VAs since that time. I based this book on my experience and theirs. One of the stumbling blocks I experienced in my journey was the lack of up-to-date and affordable resources to become a VA. There were plenty of $300 and $1,000 courses promising to teach how to become a VA, but honestly, that wasn't in my price range. I was an inner-city teacher at the time enrolled as a full-time grad student. I know that for many of you, $300 is out of your reach right now. But for those of you who are do-it-yourselfers (this is me waving to you because that's me too!), this book will help you get started with what you need to know and get your business set up in two months or less.

On my website, you'll also find resources, including videos, templates, and other tools to successfully launch your VA career. If you desire to pay down debt, start your own business, or launch your side hustle on a budget, you're in the right place. The right tools and strategies can set you up without a thousand-dollar course (and if you have that budget, you can redirect it to things like a logo or website.)

All small business owners or entrepreneurs will eventually need help organizing their online business. And due to the surge in online business and the great interest in working from home, the need for virtual assistants is more popular than ever.

The beauty of an online business is that you can manage everything digitally. Business owners don't need a local employee when an outsourced contractor who lives anywhere can be more effective in getting the job done.

The list of tasks a virtual assistant can do is endless because it varies based on individual needs. There isn't a specific list of tasks out there that business owners are supposed to outsource to a virtual assistant, and there isn't a clear list of things for a VA to accomplish to meet that task list—none of that exists. It depends on the business owner's requests.

However, many businesses share a variety of common tasks, so in this book, we'll discuss some of the more common tasks entrepreneurs hire virtual assistants for.

Many people struggle with their email inbox. (I've never been able to get to Inbox Zero in eight years of owning my business.)

A client could hire a VA to sort through their inbox, set up a system for filtering incoming messages, make sure important messages are answered, and other similar tasks. A more advanced VA—such as someone who has a customer service background—might also be suitable to respond to customers on the client's behalf.

Occasionally, a customer issue arises, or a customer complaint elevates until the business owner's attention is required. A savvy virtual assistant is the first line of defense in handling this.

But not all VA tasks are the same. Internet research is a common place where business owners and professionals need support. This could include looking for addresses, putting together a spreadsheet, reading reviews on software, and providing feedback to the client about which one seems to be the best fit.

Do you see a trend here?

Virtual assistants help get things done, which is why they're in high demand. If you enjoy overseeing projects through to their completion, this could be the perfect fit for your side hustle or even as a stay-at-home career.

In this book, you'll get an inside look at what it's like to be a virtual assistant, how to find clients and work with them effectively, and learn many of the key aspects of running a business that are critical for your success.

There is an online resource that can help you get started and implement the lessons from this book with video support and one-on-one feedback, but I'll share more about that later after you've had a chance to decide for yourself if becoming a VA is your next best step. Check out www.virtualassistantbook.com for more information and access to more materials, like templates and bonuses to help you get started as a VA. If you find it helpful, you'll be able to order a workbook to help you as you go through the chapters in this book. You'll also get a free 30-day launch calendar to help you break down this book over a one-month period.

Note: In most cases, you'll only need minimal training to get started. You might need to get up to speed with specific software or the biggest trends in digital marketing, but if you've worked in an office before, you can leverage those skills into the VA world. Even if you haven't yet worked in an office but are good with organization, filing, and helping others, those skills are enough to ease you into learning most of the other ones.

So, only one question remains: are you ready?

# 1
# WHAT IS A VA?

IF YOU WANT to work from home, you're not alone. The fact that you picked up this book shows you're looking for a flexible, freedom-based way to build your business around your life instead of your life around your business.

We live in an incredible time—with a little bit of training, passion, and effort on your part, you can set up your business online for very little money and very little risk.

Being a virtual assistant is a great way to earn extra income. Even if you already have a stable source of passive income, it's a good stay at home role to leverage for an extra bit of cash. And if you don't have a regular salary, virtual assistance is a role that you can make full-time.

The most common entry-level questions regarding VA work that I see flying around a lot are: "What is a virtual assistant?" or "what does a virtual assistant do?"

A virtual assistant is essentially a person who works from home, communicating online or over the phone (hence the virtual part) to help run an individual's blog or business. Running a business is a lot of work, so hiring someone becomes a top priority for busy entrepreneurs.

There are dozens of kinds of tasks you can offer as a virtual assistant, all of which will allow you to learn new skills or even specialize in the kinds of tasks that appeal most to you. If you've ever worked in an office or volunteered on a project where you've done administrative tasks, you can probably leverage those into a side hustle or even a full-time career as a virtual assistant.

# Is Being a VA Right for You?

Becoming a virtual assistant is a rewarding way to have a career you'll love waking up to every morning.

Before becoming a virtual assistant and freelance writer, I dreaded Mondays because that meant going back to the job I dreaded. I used to call this feeling "Sunday anxiety. "I don't miss it, and now, I enjoy waking up on Monday mornings, even after a three-week vacation so I can get back into the swing of things.

Here's what's great about being a VA—you can have any motivation for working in this field, and none of them are wrong. You can also align the size of your business with what you hope to accomplish. Need something to generate extra money that will only *cost* you five hours a week? You can do that. Want to put in the hard work to scale this to a full-time career? You can do that too.

Read on to learn four of the biggest reasons you should consider becoming a VA.

## Reason #1: Flexibility

The flexibility to work for yourself is invaluable. It gives a tremendous amount of flexibility when you're a parent, a caregiver, or are only able to contribute a few hours per day. Holding down a typical nine to five job can be frustrating and practically impossible in all these situations, but working as a virtual assistant empowers you to work on your time without any additional stress.

Unless you have scheduled calls or deadlines, most of your clients won't care if you complete the work at 2:00 a.m. or 10:00 p.m. They care about meeting deadlines, and thanks to pre-scheduling and draft tools, there are very few times you'll need to be physically present online as a virtual assistant. (Of course, clarify that's the case with all the clients you onboard!)

## Reason #2: Freedom

The number one advantage of owning my business is the freedom it allows me. What do I mean by this? My ability to choose the clients I want to work with and to turn down those who are a poor fit gives me tremendous decision-making responsibility over my day-to-day business, which also helps keep me sane.

Running an online business can quickly grow out of control if you're hiring nightmare clients or working with people who are simply too challenging. Over time, you'll grow in identifying these red flag clients before you even work together. Having this skillset will simplify your life and excite you to work each day when you have clients you care about.

## Reason #3: More Time

When you run your online business properly, every hour of work can benefit you because it'll allow you to pursue other goals. For example, as I write this book, I'm working on another book, walking five miles a day, and developing my physical endurance. None of these options were realistic for me before working online as a virtual assistant and a freelance writer.

Previously, I spent my time worrying about getting to and from work. I had to cram in all of my errands after work, which meant I exercised before I left, and had to include enough time for my commute. This juggling ate up all of my day, and I'd arrive home drained and exhausted by a meaningless job, which left me with zero motivation to work on these other issues. Now, I set up my schedule to work on my time and only select clients I truly enjoy working with.

## Reason #4: Cashing in on a Hot Opportunity

We're in a time where more people are starting online businesses. Therefore, there is more demand for help, and employers are more receptive to hiring someone to work in a virtual capacity." Entrepreneurs and bloggers have a greater knowledge of virtual assistants and their roles and are learning how much a virtual assistant can help build and grow their business.

Starting a virtual assistant business can be one of the most exciting decisions and opportunities of your life, but it can also feel overwhelming if you aren't sure what to do or what steps to take first.

The Internet is a very popular place for business today, and now more than ever, small businesses and entrepreneurs need help to accomplish their day-to-day tasks. Compared with some other freelance avenues like web design, there are fewer barriers to entry because you probably already have all the skills you need to succeed as a VA. The #1 thing I hear from other entrepreneurs in my field is they don't know where to look when they need to hire a VA! That means the demand is there.

## Five Steps to Launching a VA Career

There are five main things to keep in mind as you think about dipping your toes in the water of virtual assistant work: knowing the market, knowing your core offer, determining how much time you have to dedicate to this, focusing on clients, and getting good at conversions.

## Step #1: Know the Marketplace

There is no point in marketing yourself to potential clients if you don't know what people in the marketplace want. Doing some research helps to ground you and tell you if your idea is a good one. You want to make sure there is a demand for your particular type of offering before stepping out there and making it your thing.

It can be a big mistake to invest money and time into a website, branding, and other materials aligned with an offer no one is interested in. To get a sense of what is most popular in the world of virtual assistants today, check out popular websites like Guru, Freelancer, or Upwork.com. You'll see plenty of job bids posting information about virtual assistants and what types of services are most in-demand.

From my experience, the following are the services that can make a virtual assistant practically irresistible to hire:

- Social media management

- WordPress management and content marketing management

- Personal life management including scheduling, completing travel requirements, and other personal details

- Online research

- Advanced software tools like Mailchimp, Constant Contact, Keap, ConvertKit

There are many different types of tasks a virtual assistant can do, so you need to match your skillset with marketplace's demand. This is the best way to identify how to get started.

## Step #2: Determine Your Core Offer

Some individuals focus specifically on one particular industry, such as serving solo entrepreneurs with online businesses. Others might choose only to handle specific tasks. For example, some virtual assistants are experts with Pinterest and other social media strategies. Others are skilled in online research or related aspects of their business.

You can certainly be a generalist and accomplish many of these tasks at once. Still, it can also be beneficial to strategize and narrow your market to a particular industry or type of project you'll focus on. As you grow in experience in these various categories, you'll determine what you like and don't like, which can help you refine your decision about the services you'll offer. Think about your core offer and how you'll work—by project or on an hourly basis.

Most virtual assistants start on an hourly basis, and it can be beneficial for you when you're not yet sure how long it takes you to do certain projects. Some clients, however, prefer to pay a flat rate per project instead of hourly. For example, a social media manager might offer a flat rate service of several hundred dollars per month for basic social media. However, they may also do other virtual assistant tasks on an hourly basis. It's important to think about whether you want to keep track of your hours and pitch yourself as an hourly virtual assistant.

## Step #3: Identify Your Time Commitment

This is one of the most important aspects of setting up your virtual business. You need to think carefully about whether you want to work part-time or full-time and how many hours you can dedicate. In the beginning, you'll spend a significant amount of time doing marketing work instead of working for clients. This means you'll be doing a lot of what's known as "unbillable hours. "These unbillable hours are necessary to build your client base.

As you grow and build your client base, this will change. You'll spend less time on marketing and more time working for clients. Ideally, your good impression upon your current clients has led them to refer you to others or booked yourself up so much you don't need to market.

In the beginning, however, you need to set aside specific goals associated with your marketing. For example, you might spend a couple of hours per week marketing your services like making phone calls, sending emails, visiting job boards, or blogging on your website to attract clients. You also want to be realistic about the time you can dedicate to create and deliver client work. Falling behind and missing deadlines is the number one way to push a current client away.

Do you only have two hours per week? You probably won't be able to work on many projects. However, if you have ten hours per week, you can spend those first couple of weeks pitching and trying to land clients and then switching over to spend as many of those ten hours on client projects as possible.

## Step #4: Focus in on Clients

One great way to start your virtual assistant business is to think about how many clients you want to work with and who they are. A lot of little projects can add up to a lucrative career as a virtual assistant, but it can also be overwhelming to track all of these various client needs. For example, you might prefer to work with a handful of in-depth clients. Think carefully about how often you interact with these clients.

Working for one major client with a very high-value contract could mean that you need to touch base with this person every day. Is this something you desire or have time for? Also, think about where these clients are coming from. How are they being introduced to your world? Do you have a marketing system set up to bring them in regularly?

Considering your ideal client will help you identify someone who is a perfect fit for you as opposed to someone who doesn't belong on your client roster.

## Step #5: Be Prepared to Close the Sale

Even with the most excellent marketing in the world, it can be difficult to ask for the sale. Far too many people never get to this point in their business without a little bit of anxiety. Be prepared to offer hourly or per-project packages. Consulting with a client and asking for the sale on the phone means you need to be confident about your services and the offers you provide.

To pitch a client and have them ready to accept your offer, you must be clear about several things:

- Will you charge hourly or based on a package?

- What will your rates be?

- How much time will you dedicate to your clients' goals?

- What kind of projects do you enjoy the most?

Don't worry that you don't have this information yet! Reading this book will help you get there.

A client should always feel excited at the end of an email exchange or phone call with you to discuss the potential to work together.

As you build and grow your virtual assistant career, you'll learn a lot along the way. You can use these steps to determine what type of VA you want to be to begin making offers to clients!

If you're still not sure what you should offer yet, don't fear. Begin by researching your field of interest to help you think about the prospective services you can offer. Before you go on to the next chapter, set aside some time to research other virtual assistants. This is a great way to get those creative juices flowing!

## What You Can Learn from Other Successful VAs

When you're completely new as a virtual assistant, I commonly see people fall into the "compare and despair" trap. In this situation, the success of other VAs intimidates you into thinking you can't make it work as well as they have. Well, my friend, if you're dedicated to being a success, you absolutely can. There's plenty of room for qualified VAs—many of the best ones are in high demand. One of the first VAs I ever worked with in my business booked up in less than two months when she was brand new! You can do it too!

While you don't want to spend too much time thinking about others, you can use this research in your favor. Learning from others is a great way to avoid re-inventing the wheel. When I first launched my freelance business, I spent time looking into my competitors to figure out how I could do what they were doing better. You can learn a lot from successful VAs. This is even more true if they have a blog detailing their experience.

Many people get overwhelmed when launching a new VA business because it seems like there are so many tough decisions to make. That's why I encourage you not to make all the decisions on your own. For example, you can lose hours of valuable time trying to decide if you should have a blog. It's much easier to do some market research and determine what's working for others and whether it's worth your time. Successful VAs can teach you a lot about what you need to know.

Instead of comparing yourself with other successful VAs, make a note of their names and websites. Then, carve out an hour or two when you can study their websites and get a feel for how they work. These materials can help you refine your offerings and figure out how you're different so you can stand out from the crowd.

Get started by doing a Google search for VAs to see some of your competition. Then, begin the research process.

Someone else's practices can help you, but remember, it's not a good idea to copy someone else. Instead, use the knowledge to craft your unique value proposition for clients. Other VA websites can tell you what you should or shouldn't share on your site. This is a powerful exercise because you'll probably spot trends. For example, you might see many VAs offer a broad range of services, while some choose to specialize in email marketing or some other niche task type. You can get a sense of what appeals to you by looking at other people.

Here are a couple of things you'll want to look at in your research:

- The style of the site

- How the person encourages potential clients to get in touch

- Whether their rates are listed and whether or not these are hourly or package-based

- The general tone and style of the person's writing. Fun? Professional? Dedicated?

- The kinds of services the VA offers.

To make things simple, **I created a basic spreadsheet (www. bit.ly/vaspreadsheet)** where you can keep track of your competitors' research. It's view-only so everyone can use it, but you can download it as an Excel file or select *File*, then *Make a copy*. Having all this info in front of you can help you determine what's popular in the VA world (i.e. rates, a certain type of offering, etc.) and help you figure out how to refine your unique business.

My goal in writing this book is to introduce you to the available opportunities working as a virtual assistant, to showcase some of the tips and tricks that will help you get started and some of the most common pitfalls to avoid, and insights from other virtual assistants to help you see how you can build that for yourself. You might be able to read this book in one sitting, but you'll get far more out of it if you work on one chapter a day and take notes.

Now that you know what it looks like to be a VA, it's time to think about some of the specifics around your VA business and what you should know before you launch!

# 2
# WOULD YOU MAKE A GOOD VIRTUAL ASSISTANT?

BEFORE YOU GO too deep into deciding whether to make a real go of working as a virtual assistant, let's talk about the reality of it. In this chapter, you'll learn more about some of the personality traits and preferences that will enable your success as a VA. But, the absence of a few traits doesn't mean you'll automatically fail. Instead, use the information in this chapter to boost your confidence.

It's a misconception to suggest you have to enter VA work with certifications, training, or degrees. What's most important as a virtual assistant is your ability to keep track of multiple projects at the same time, your desire to learn, and some organization/tech-savvy ability. But it does help if you come to the table with some of the proven skills necessary to be a successful virtual assistant.

One of the most common concerns for people considering becoming a virtual assistant is a worry that they don't have enough experience or training to succeed. However, the chances are good that there is plenty of experience in your background to help you work as a virtual assistant. Even if you've never worked remotely or aren't familiar with the software used in online marketing, your passion for learning and a desire to succeed can help you overcome some of these challenges.

## A Case Study: My Journey into Becoming a VA

Let's look at my background to explore how experience can directly relate to virtual assistant work even when if it doesn't appear similar.

The first time I was paid for online work was with my job as a virtual assistant. I had a master's degree in political science, worked as a receptionist at an insurance agency, had plenty of experience working in law firms, and worked as a teaching assistant while earning my master's degree. There are many different skills from all of those different jobs that help me succeed as a virtual assistant and as a freelancer. For example, working as a receptionist at an insurance agency and in law offices often required me to handle multiple projects simultaneously. I faced constant disruption with questions, ringing phones, or emails. The ability to balance multiple projects definitely helps when working as a virtual assistant and servicing multiple clients simultaneously.

Furthermore, all of my experience working as a teacher helped me to provide people with feedback. My ability to break down bigger projects into smaller steps and help people navigate some of their obstacles while working through projects was a learned, invaluable skill I could tap into as a virtual assistant. For my clients, I frequently had to explain things and decide how to break down bigger projects like launching a website or starting an email list for them.

Analyzing your past skills as a homemaker, volunteer, or employee in Corporate America, or as an entrepreneur running a business can all serve to help you to identify the skill sets relatable to your potential virtual assistant clients. Even if it doesn't seem as though you have many of the skills successful virtual assistants have, pull together a list of some of the most effective communication, organization, and project management skills that will serve you well as a virtual assistant.

# What Skills Do Successful VAs Need?

These are some of the skills that will make your transition into online work easier and more successful.

## *Time Management*

As a VA, you'll likely juggle tasks for multiple clients simultaneously. You'll also have to set up your schedule for administrative and marketing work. It helps if you know how to plot out the necessary time to work on your business and can estimate how long certain tasks might take.

If you already have a job, fitting in your VA work around your family, personal life, and job might be a challenge. You might only have five or ten hours at a time to dedicate to your business each week, so you have to be smart about how to spend that time. As your business grows, you'll spend less of your time marketing and searching for clients and more time working on projects, but those time management skills will remain important.

## *Interpersonal Skills*

Remember that your clients are hiring someone to help them with their business. Even though you'll be an outsider to their company, their company is probably very personal to the client.

Since you'll be stepping into their business and interfacing with the client online, interpersonal skills can go a long way toward breaking down communication barriers. The easier it is for you to ask questions, clarify concerns, and address mistakes, the more likely you'll build long-term relationships with clients. They'll be thrilled to provide you with testimonials, referrals, and ongoing work down the road!

Being a great communicator goes a long way in any business, but it's even more important in the digital age when we rely on short voice messages, texts, and emails more than ever.

## Internet and Computer Skills

If you're not feeling especially tech savvy, the good news is that there are many free or affordable platforms today to learn new technology. (There's a future chapter dedicated to some of the most in-demand software tools and how to find training for them coming your way.)

However, you should be able to navigate your way around websites, manage documents and spreadsheets, and know how to use Microsoft Word. If you've been a student, volunteer, or employee in the past ten years, you probably have all the basic tools needed to get started as a VA. Growing as a VA with your technical skills is easier than ever, thanks to the Internet, and you can always learn by doing as you implement marketing technology for your own VA business.

## Organizational Skills

Most business owners arrive in your inbox because they feel overwhelmed and need organizational help. They might be planning to work with you to get their organization and filing back on track, so if organization is one of your strongest skillsets, you can leverage this to land and keep clients.

Arriving with ideas about systems and strategy will go a long way in making your clients excited to work with you and will ultimately help their success too! These are the biggest reasons why it's so important to have these skills already.

## Resourceful

Perhaps what your client needs is a big investment in their software, but they can't quite afford it. It might be up to you to help figure out alternatives to at least buffer the client until their revenue is higher, and you can reopen that discussion. Being resourceful and knowing where to find information is a key skill for any VA.

I tasked one of my VAs with finding new webinar software. Frustrated with the constant bugs and problems we experienced with the current software, I shared my budget with her and gave my parameters like a long trial period so I could make a decision after using the product. She created a master spreadsheet based on cost, features, and online reviews that helped me decide. This is important because your clients don't always expect you to have all the answers. But being resourceful and knowing where to look for some answers is as helpful.

## Follow-through and Follow-up

Seeing a project from beginning to end is exciting for some people and boring for others. Along the way, there are many details to track. If you're the type of person who loses steam midway through a project or gets frazzled when you hit your first obstacle, working as a VA might be a challenge for you. From following up with clients you previously pitched to gently nudging that current client for the password you need to finish the job, it's up to you to make sure nothing slips through the cracks. Your clients will thank you for it!

## Creative Thinking & Problem-Solving Skills

Are you an idea generator? Are your friends always coming to you because you have creative solutions to fixing problems or for a new and fresh approach? You're a business owner's dream!

There's no doubt that you'll encounter roadblocks to getting a project done. What makes virtual assistants such valuable assets to their clients is that they don't see problems like traffic jams. Instead, VAs see problems as opportunities because they like navigating these challenges.

Over the past few years, I have had the opportunity to work with freelancers like graphic designers, virtual assistants, web developers, and writers who want to grow their businesses more quickly and effectively. One of the most common questions I receive from new and emerging virtual assistants I work with is how they can offer extreme value to VA clients. If you're new to the virtual assistant world, you probably have questions about what your client is looking for and how you can go above and beyond to build a long-term relationship with them. It's a lot easier than you think.

## Ability to Handle Difficult Situations

While there are potential virtual assistants who'll provide you with outstanding opportunities and great communication skills, you can't always count on this as a virtual assistant. Even implementing the best screening as an entrepreneur won't block every red flag client from working with you. As a virtual assistant, sometimes you have to be a truth-teller and tell your client difficult news. However, if you have expertise in an area the client doesn't, it's much more important to be honest upfront and help the client get the best result.

In other situations, you'll need to notify those clients who are pushing your working relationship's boundaries. These are never easy conversations to have—we'll explore this in more detail in this book's client management section. You must be prepared to have these conversations to protect your boundaries and integrity. Your willingness to step up to the plate can also repel those clients who might take advantage of your generous and giving nature.

# Personality Traits that Will Help a VA

While anyone who has the drive and basic skills can do well as a VA, the business of working for yourself while providing services to others mean that certain personality traits will make this easier for you.

## You Love Managing Yourself

If you enjoy seeing a task through to completion, you may find success as a virtual assistant. The client's primary goal in giving their VA a project is to take it off of their plate and for you to see that it gets done.

If you love working on deadlines and for yourself, then being a virtual assistant may work out extremely well for you because you won't have to rely on too many other individuals to succeed in this role. You'll need clear instructions from the person who hired you and the ability to carry out your responsibilities.

But you won't have to count on co-workers to show up to meetings on time. You may love a career as a VA if you work well on your own and enjoy your autonomy.

## You Aren't Afraid to Continue Working When You Make a Mistake

If you find yourself easily derailed by problems, annoying people, a lack of organization, or sometimes longer days, then being a virtual assistant may not be for you.

Someone who succeeds in the virtual assistant role is likely able to adapt easily and quickly to a variety of situations. He or she always knows what's going on with numerous different projects and understands the next step necessary to move the projects forward.

## Ability and Willingness to Market

It's unlikely you'll set up a website as a virtual assistant and land your first contract immediately. You're going to have to do some legwork to promote yourself, not just now, but well into the future. Once you have a couple of satisfied clients, you may find that your calendar is full, or they refer you to others, and you don't have to do as much marketing.

But you must be willing to constantly determine whether your marketing plan is working to onboard new clients. You must be crystal clear about your offerings, ready to do consultations that may not result in a sale, and constantly offer services high demand services. You must be able to adapt and put yourself out there to make phone calls, do interviews, and solicit clients directly. This job isn't for the faint of heart. Simply setting up a website and calling yourself a virtual assistant doesn't guarantee you'll have a contract. Instead, you have to put in the legwork and ensure that you're constantly working on effective strategies to bring on clients, which means doing outreach and pitches every single week.

## Like Working by Yourself

One of the most challenging things about running your own business is how much it falls in your lap. This means that you're the driving force behind everything, and your commitment and schedule will match that. While you might bring on subcontractors or run your business as an agency or a solopreneur, you'll still be doing a lot of the work on your own.

There's no doubt that you might be able to break up all the individual work by partnering with others, doing video calls with clients, or even venturing out to a coffee shop from time to time. But most of the work in running any freelance business has to do with you.

For some people, this can be way too isolating. If you're an introvert who never loved office politics and the constant disruptions of your co-worker smacking gum, you might love it. You might find that you're far more focused and productive when you're alone.

Even as an introvert, I find that it's still a good idea for me to network at least once a week. For that reason, I always schedule calls, do live videos, offer free training, take dance classes, or have coffee chats with people online that I'm getting to know. Even during my long Minnesota winters, this helps me feel like I'm getting out and about even if that isn't physically possible.

## Love Learning and Helping Others

After leaving a career as a teacher, I instantly saw that one thing I liked about being in the freelance space was the opportunity to help other people with their business. I got to peek behind the curtain to see what other people were doing best and learn new skills and tools along the way.

Plus, when something went well in their business that I'd helped with, it felt like a win for me too! When I got all the tech to work, and they had a sold-out webinar, I felt like I was a part of that team. Even as you're growing your business as a VA, you should always keep your client's needs and interests first, and you should be excited about being able to help them grow too!

## Enjoy a Flexible Schedule

Some people prefer to have a set schedule and a roadmap for the days and weeks where there is already a routine. That's going to be very hard to achieve as a virtual assistant because you'll have clients coming and going, projects ranging in priority, and busy times and slow times. Perhaps the VAs best secret weapon is that they can dive in and out of projects and can work 40 hours one week due to launch and not panic when the next week is only ten hours of work (assuming, of course, you're getting paid fairly for all your work!)

## Like Creating Your Own Paycheck

In college and graduate school, there were multiple times I worked on commission. Some days I had to make a certain quota to keep my job. I thrived under that pressure and mostly saw the upside to make as much money as possible through my commission; I never let the downside freak me out much. You might do well in that kind of environment, too, but not if you're the kind of person who needs to know where every single dollar is coming from and where it's going.

As a self-employed business owner for the past eight years, I've always enjoyed setting my rate and taking accountability for my work in generating my paycheck.

The downside is if you slack off or are too busy with client work and forget to do your marketing, that's on you. There's no regular paycheck dropping into your account, so you have to work hard to make sure you've kept cash flow moving.

## A Day in the Life of a VA

It's mentioned in a few different ways above but working as a VA requires flexibility and the ability to handle multiple projects simultaneously. What follows is just an example of what your day might look like if you have a handful of clients but have not scaled to a full-time business yet.

9:00 a.m. to 10:00 a.m.: Check emails, and make sure there are no fires to put out. Then, check out prominent job boards and "Facebook groups" to see if any new leads have posted.

10:00 a.m. to 10:30 a.m.: Brainstorm marketing message for the day. Post on social media.

10:30 a.m. to 12:00 p.m.: Working on client projects

12:00 p.m. to 1:00 p.m.: Lunch break

1:00 p.m. to 2:00 p.m.: New prospective client calls and proposal writing

2:00 p.m. to 5:00 p.m.: Client work; send invoices and invoice reminders

Of course, you don't have to use a 9-5 model, but since most of your clients will work a typical workday, it's good to have some solid hours that overlap with that time. By all means, if you're more focused in the morning and essentially brain dead after 3:00 p.m. (that'd be me, folks) you can wake up early and work on client projects and marketing and not take any calls after 3:00 p.m. You get to decide. Having some form of office hours makes it easier for people to reach you, makes it simpler to schedule childcare, and helps you stay consistent.

When I first started working from home full-time, I resisted the idea of having a full eight-hour workday. I wanted to rebel against the system I'd hated so much. But I found that being too flexible, like sleeping until 11:00 a.m., actually made me feel more stressed out and overwhelmed. It was much easier to keep a generally consistent schedule with some room for flexibility like an afternoon off or lunch with my husband or a friend.

When you first start your business, you'll be a solopreneur by default unless you join another agency of VAs. It's important to recognize that many of these positions aren't independent contractors and come with set rates. In a VA agency, someone running the company will contract you out to various clients either focused mostly on one client or being shared on many different projects. The agency will almost always set the rates, and you'll need to comply with their schedule expectations. This can be a good way to break into the marketplace and get some experience as a new VA if you're too nervous about finding clients.

However, I encourage you to branch out as soon as possible unless you love the agency you're working with. It's hard to feel a part of the bigger vision in many cases, the rates paid at most agencies are below what you could earn on your own, and you'll need to follow what agency rules and guidelines are. Simply put, you don't have much ability to call the shots, which is why many VAs eventually start out on their own.

You can check out the resource website for this book and download Handout #1, Agencies Hiring VAs, to see an up to date version of companies that accept new applicants.

No matter what you choose, there is no wrong answer. Either way, you have the option to get some experience and earn extra money.

## Your Next Step: Take a Skills Inventory

If you're convinced this opportunity is right for you but are still wondering how to use your skills and interests to pursue your offer, read on. The perfect place to start is a skills inventory.

A skills inventory involves listing everything you know how to do that could be done remotely. A good starting place is your computer skills. Whether it's Microsoft Office, Adobe, Google Drive, or more, start listing out all the familiar things.

Make a comprehensive list and add on some general tasks like communicating with customers or answering emails. If you were trained by someone on their processes for this, how comfortable would you feel doing it? And you're probably going to come up with a pretty big list. What I encourage you to do is stop at this particular point in the module, press pause on the video, and start making a major list. And it's something that you may add to over a couple of days because more will occur to you.

Give yourself some time to make this master list, ideally in a day or two. You can start the list today after completing this chapter and revisit it as you work through other sections of the book and have new ideas.

Include all your current skills on this list, even new ones.

When you're done, you're going to update the list into stoplight colors. From here, color each of those tasks green, yellow, or red:

- Green: I'm completely confident in my ability to do this task today with minor instructions from my client.

- Yellow: I'm somewhat comfortable with this, but I need more training.

- Red: I know next to nothing about this, and it would be a significant hurdle for me to learn this.

The initial ones to focus on are the ones you colored green and yellow, especially if they're already tasks you enjoy.

In this chapter, we covered how to know this line of work is a good fit for you. In the next chapter, you'll learn how to set goals for your new virtual assistant business.

# 3
# HOW TO GET STARTED

BEFORE KICKING OFF a career as a virtual assistant, you need to consider why you want a VA career. Ultimately, this is a personal decision, but it could be for one or a combination of the following reasons:

- Working toward more freedom and flexibility

- Knowing that your skillset matches with the industry needs

- Wanting more money while staying at your job part time or even full time

- Hoping to transition from a job that you work outside the home to working at home either part-time or full-time

- Wanting to experience something new every day

- Looking to expand your skillset

Wanting to generate new forms of income to pay down debt or accomplish new goals for your family, like making investments or renovating.

Take a couple of minutes and think about the main reasons why you're taking this course. What do you hope to get out of it? Why do you want to become a virtual assistant? Understanding your why is essential in moving forward so that you can feel confident about your decision and reflect upon it when you're facing challenges launching your new business.

## The Why Matters for New VAs

It's important to know your reason why, because sometimes, virtual assistant or other freelancer expectations don't line up with reality. If you're looking for a quick buck or a get-rich-quick job, those aren't the right motivation to start your career as a VA because you'll find yourself quickly frustrated. The same goes for the desire to rush to get out of your current job ASAP.

While I certainly understand why you feel this way and have been there myself, this shouldn't be your primary motivation for starting a career as a VA. You might rush through some of the aspects of this book or try to lock in a client as soon as possible without really thinking about whether that person is the right fit for you. The best way I can recommend handling the transition from your current job to work from home as a virtual assistant is to set a timeline to transition out of your current job. You don't want to burn bridges or leave your full-time job before you're too confident in your ability to replicate or exceed that income at home. So, take it with a grain of salt. It might be difficult to stay with your current job but know that you're working toward a bigger goal.

If you're hoping to find an opportunity that takes very little or no effort on your part, you're going to struggle as a virtual assistant. I've talked about the value of a virtual assistant and what role he or she plays for a business owner or entrepreneur. Hoping to do something quickly and make a lot of money is going to mean that you'll have a very difficult time as a virtual assistant, and you probably won't attract the right type of clients, either.

It's also a mistake to assume that you'll never confront any challenges. Even the most experienced individuals following all of the right steps will make mistakes because we're human.

What makes you different is committing to this program of overcoming those challenges and confronting them head-on. No one expects you to be perfect, and nobody in business is perfect, but you need to allow yourself to overcome these challenges when they're coming at you.

Whenever you encounter a challenge on the job as a VA, reflect back on your reasons for getting started to keep you motivated. There's a reason many people compare owning a business to a rollercoaster—some days it's up, and some days it's down.

Some days you may accomplish major marketing goals or bring on an incredible new client, but this isn't always the case. You need to be prepared to move forward with momentum as much as possible, even if it's only baby steps.

## Setting the Right Goals

Your first three months may be the most difficult. I recommend setting a reasonable goal you can achieve. For some people, that might be $200 a month. For those of you who don't have other full-time obligations, that could be $500 a month or more. Or perhaps you want to save a certain amount of money to start putting it in the cushion for when you leave your full-time job. Whatever that is, have a specific amount of money you're working toward, and keep reflecting on this piece of paper. Keep checking in where you're at and celebrate those small wins.

If you book $200 in business for that very first month and accomplish that in the first two weeks, you deserve to celebrate, and it might be a good opportunity to recalibrate your goals too. You might think, *Hey, if I did meet my goal in half the time I thought I would, maybe it's time to reconsider it and make that goal even bigger.* After this initial three-month period is where I really encourage you to be consistent with your marketing and work to bring on full-time clients or add a new client every month.

## Verify Your Family's Onboard with Your Why

Another important thing concerning logistics is whether your family members are on board with the idea and your new schedule and commitments.

This can be a huge challenge anytime you start an at-home business. A lot of people don't understand what it's like to run an at-home business. It doesn't mean that you can always do everything in your free time; you may have appointments and schedules to keep, but getting family members on board with that and respecting the boundaries can be challenging.

If you have children, it's a good idea to keep your working hours while they're at school, assuming they attend school out of the home. This means that you can get as much done as possible and arrange your schedule around their needs. It also helps you optimize your work so that what you're working on while they're at school are the tasks that require most of your focus and attention.

It is definitely worth having a conversation with them to say you're working and appreciate their support. And it's trial and error with the timing at first, but you'll find what works for you.

A week or two into marketing, tasks, and pitching to potential clients will tell you whether you need to have another conversation with your family members or whether you're in a good position to move forward.

## Setting Working Hours

The idea of set working hours doesn't work for everyone, but you do need a schedule.

Most people don't choose to be a virtual assistant to recreate their day job at home, and there's also been plenty of studies showing that your productivity drops off after about 30 or 40 hours of working per week on something. If you're good at treating it like it's an appointment or a class, that can motivate you to get it done and to stay consistent with it.

Over time you'll learn when your most productive hours are, where you work the best, and you'll also learn how long you need to commit to particular projects where you're still being productive and enjoying yourself. This is why the process of goal setting factors into this equation. You have to have faith in your goals and the concept that you're working toward something bigger. Sometimes, the smaller, mundane tasks you're working on can feel frustrating as you're going through the process.

## Setting a Goal for What You Want to Accomplish as a VA

One of the most important ways to succeed from the beginning of a virtual assisting career is by planning because working backward to accomplish your goals will increase the chances that you'll achieve them.

One commonality among successful VAs is the strong desire to leave their current jobs. So, in working backward, it's a good idea to plan to leave your job within six to 12 months of launching your virtual assistant career.

First, you need to build up a financial cushion to support you when you first leap. Second, you must mentally have a financial goal in mind that'll allow you to leave your job with less stress and concern about finances. Having a certain number of clients already or steady business for several months can make you feel better about making that jump. So, there are pros of leaving your job early. Some people try to target the date for leaving their full-time job to be around six months. There are some advantages associated with this. Mostly, it can relieve a lot of the stress you're feeling in your day job. It can also be exciting as you recommit to your business on a deeper level. When you're unconcerned about jumping from job to job and you've already established some key clients and enough income to be picky about your clients, you can have a big advantage if you have a financial cushion. However, it's not always the right choice to leave your job earlier rather than later. You need to carefully evaluate your income over several months and keep track of the hours you're working the business through marketing and client work.

If you don't have the financial support in place to get you through this difficult time, you're going to scramble for business. That puts a lot of pressure on you, and it means you're more likely to take on contracts that aren't a good fit for you. And also, it can really leave you in the lurch. Sometimes it happens without you planning for it, and perhaps you've been laid off or fired or couldn't handle it one more day there, so you quit. That could prompt you to work harder than ever to get your business on track, but I don't recommend doing this unless you've carefully thought about it. You always want to be working backward toward these goals you set with the intentions sheet. So, what is the monthly dollar amount you'll feel comfortable receiving each month that would allow you the peace of mind to leave your day job?

It's also important to factor in where you're going to work. Do you have sufficient space at home to do this full time? How is this going to influence your tax situation? There are a lot of implications to think about, and that's why I encourage people to take a couple of months to consider it before making the jump to do this full time. If it fits into your life really well as a part-time endeavor, that can allow you to build up some experience and testimonials from clients and finances and confidence to go from part time to full time. So, before you set your goal about whether you'd like to leave your job and when you'd like that to happen, what was the number goal you already set for yourself? Is it $2,000 a month? $3,000? $5,000? And are you still committed to that?

And along with that, it's not just the goal of the finances that you need, it's also to carefully consider how much time you're going to commit and marketing effort you're going to commit to bringing in clients. So, it's possible that even in-between the first module and the second module, life got in the way, and you didn't accomplish some of the goals you wanted to. This is a good chance to recommit and reconsider if you have the same hours set aside every week to working with clients and marketing your business. You might need to readjust those expectations. Income goals are really important in figuring out what money you're going to bring in and at what point you can go from part-time to full time.

Let's look at an example here. Always do the math backward. This is why setting those goals is achievable when you break it into pieces. So, let's imagine you're going to pitch yourself as a virtual assistant for $20 an hour, which is perfectly reasonable for an experienced virtual assistant. A less experienced virtual assistant might want to adjust that rate lower to begin. Imagine that your initial target in your first couple of months is $400. For some people, especially if they already have a full-time job, this would be a great side income to save or scale into a full-time income down the road. But $400 a month is achievable and equates to five working hours per week. That's different than total hours because you're going to do a fair amount of marketing and administrative things in your business to get set up. You could probably fit this into your schedule even if you have a part-time or full-time job elsewhere. You could spend two or three hours on a Saturday and space it out for the rest of the week. $400 a month in revenue isn't profit because you're going to spend time doing other marketing activities, and you may have other investments. But it's really good to think about these numbers because when you have a specific number goal, and you're working toward it, everything that motivates you that month should be to get you to that monthly goal. Break that down into an hourly rate, and then it becomes much more achievable to think you need a client to pay you for five hours a week, which is doable and achievable with only one or two clients.

You'll probably need to commit at least twice as much time to marketing in the beginning because you don't have clients yet. But once you have that initial client or two, you want to be getting paid for five working hours a week. So, if you're aiming for that, then you'd want to aim for ten total, and you'll spend the rest of those doing administrative tasks and marketing to grow your business.

When you think about leaving your day job, it's really important to outline an exit strategy. While you don't necessarily need one and not everyone will use one, some people need to exit their job sooner rather than later. They won't have plans in place for it, and that's okay. It's a little bit more challenging if you do it this way, but having an exit strategy can also help you mentally when you're having a difficult day at work. It's good to know you're building something at home that could ultimately replace or even exceed your day job income. So, it's a good motivator, and it's also professional because there's no need to burn bridges unless you have to. So, perhaps your exit strategy looks something like this: the first three months that you commit to working as a virtual assistant, you're making $400 a month in revenue. And if possible, take all of what's left over after your expenses and save it. It should be relatively easy to scale that to $800 a month in months three to six because you'll have ideally expanded those existing contracts with your current clients or brought on new clients.

If you're using the 12-month exit strategy, then after month six, aim for $1000 or more per month. And again, happy clients mean referrals, and if you're to the point of turning down business or being so busy that you can't respond to everybody, you're definitely in this sweet spot. So, this allows you to save some money and gives you peace of mind. It instills confidence in you to make money outside of your day job because if you're good at saving it, you've got a cushion where you think, *Well, if I leave my job and this flops, I've got at least 3 to 6 months of savings already in the bank.* It gives you some opportunities. Now, very rarely will people need that because if you're like me, when I went from part-time to full time, I tripled my revenue. Previously, I'd only been able to work ten or 15 hours a week, and now I worked 30 or 40. It grew dramatically from there. That internal confidence that comes with knowing you have a cushion almost gives you the permission to try something new like leaving your day job. And I don't think it's negative to think you have a couple months saved up even if things don't work out.

You almost need to permit yourself to leave your day job in some circumstances. It's not going to be easy even if you're fed up and frustrated, so having some money saved and a growing business can help. Another way to simply break this down is to think when you have X dollars saved and X steady clients, you'll be ready to leave your job. Now, write that down and really dedicate yourself to that because, again, permission to achieve something and move on is important. I can tell you it's hard to leave your day job, even if you've met this goal. When I surpassed my day job income in just three months, I stayed at that company for another nine months because I wasn't sure if the rug was going to be pulled out from under my feet. I wanted to have a year's worth of income to see what the fluctuations and seasons were, if there was a specific amount I could count on every month, or other things I'd need to be aware of going forward. And only at that point did I truly feel ready to work for myself full time. Be patient with yourself; you may have the same experience, or it might be easier for you. You might leave your job sooner than you expected, but having financial goals in mind of what you're going to make in your first 12 months, what amount you'd like to save, and the amount of clients you'd like to have is really good for your self-esteem and your confidence moving forward.

Now, some people at this point in the module might say they don't want to leave their job and are looking for a legitimate part-time income. There's nothing wrong with that, and you're certainly not alone. But these money strategies are still really important for you because they're going to give you a better sense of what you're working toward accomplishing.

It's really easy to give up, feel frustrated, be very busy, and not really stick to your goals. But having these money strategies in place is as important whether you intend to leave your job or not because you're constantly going to be evaluating your status.

Staying accountable with your goals is critical in all aspects of business whether you intend to pursue this part time or full time.

Once you've developed those short-term financial goals, you also want to think about your long term financial goals. This goes back to the intentions sheet you completed in module one. It can be really empowering to create a vision board for these bigger goals. What is the real reason you became a virtual assistant? Some of it might have to be with the actual work environment itself, such as working for yourself and not going to the office anymore. But you might hope to go on vacation, have a better Christmas for the kids next year, buy a new car, pay down debt, replace a day job income, and more. Put that on a vision board.

A vision board keeps you accountable. It serves to remind you during the exhausting days of marketing, rough client experiences, or lack of clients that your reason and your why is critical and brought you here.

In this chapter, we talked about your why and how to set goals. In the next chapter, we're driving into the logistics of starting your business.

# 4
# WHAT YOU NEED TO GET STARTED

WHEN YOU HAVE all your ducks in a row and feel confident that you've done some initial work to kickstart your business, you'll feel more excited to start pitching to clients. In this chapter, we'll cover the basics that you must have and some optional things that will make your life easier. There are plenty of things to keep in mind when starting your virtual assistant business, so let's dive right in.

## Your Home Office

The first thing to ask yourself is if you have a dedicated place to work. It doesn't have to be large or your ideal home office. The space simply needs to be quiet, where you can keep some of the important papers and related tools like your computer, scanner/printer, and perhaps a business phone line.

While you don't need a lot of space, it's a really good idea to carve about a specific area to do this work. Take some time to consider when and where you're going to do this work because separating personal and business space is important.

Even if it's a small area, it should be somewhere where you can do your work easily. Keep in mind the foot traffic that's coming in and out of those areas. Are you going to be able to work quietly and get tasks done? Also, think about factoring in good lighting and the ability to have peace and quiet.

## A Decent Tech Stack

At a bare minimum, you'll need a computer, a phone, a webcam, a microphone or headset, and a good Internet connection. It also helps to be familiar with the Microsoft Suite of products, since these are most commonly used. While you can learn other software and tools as needed, this is a great place to start to keep your expenses and learning curve minimal when you begin.

## A Marketing Plan

We'll talk more about getting paid—everyone's favorite subject —in Chapter 8. For now, know that you'll need a marketing plan or some clear goals to help you reach out to new clients. As part of that marketing plan, you'll also need a few things:

- A good pitch
- Profiles on job board sites
- A good LinkedIn profile
- A basic website/portfolio
- Materials to take clients to the next level when they're interested, such as contracts, invoices, and proposal templates.

# Busting Common Myths about Being a VA

Even if you currently don't believe any of the below myths, you might encounter prospective clients or people in the online world who don't understand what you do. Ensure you're clear about these VA myths and be prepared to speak to them as you address the difficult situations referenced in Chapter 2.

## Most Jobs Are Scams

There are certainly scams out there, but they're easy to spot if you know what you're looking for. Here are a few quick tips to spot scams:

- If the client won't talk to you over a video call, it's probably a scam. Google Hangouts is a commonplace for scammers to hang out. If they won't communicate with you any other way, there's an issue.

- If it sounds too good to be true, it probably is. If you're being promised $400/week for generic "admin" or "book-keeping "tasks, it's probably not real. Be especially wary of gigs asking you to mail things or receive packages on behalf of the owner.

- If the client asks you to buy anything (printer, computer, etc.) before you start working, it's probably a scam. This is also true if they ask you to Western Union them the money for this alleged equipment.

- If the client asks you to send your bank account details, this one gets tricky. Many legitimate companies pay over ACH, but if you're nervous, ask for your first payment to be made in another manner until it feels it's legit.

VAs Just Sell Hours

The pricing chapter in this book will provide many different ways to get paid for your virtual assistant work. One of these is through an hourly rate. Whether you're selling blocks of hours and discounting the average hourly rate in those blocks based on the client's purchase, or, if you're invoicing clients after you had an opportunity to do the work, this is one option available to you.

However, many virtual assistants ultimately transition over to working on a retainer or project basis. For example, one of my virtual assistants receives a monthly retainer for all the work that he completes. Sometimes, the work in a given month is greater than the month before, but we've worked together long enough to know that most of it comes out in the wash. He also knows to inform me if his workload is too much for his retainer and to renegotiate it into a higher rate.

## VAs Do Everything

One of the most common misconceptions is that there is one magic unicorn out. This unicorn can handle every single task the entrepreneur needs. But more often than not, most virtual assistants thrive in handling three to five total tasks. Well, they might be able to handle more than that; some of these other tasks might not be in their zone of genius. Your client's zone of genius is what they and only they can do best. This means that plenty of other tasks they might be doing already could be transferred over to you instead! Just like your client, you have a zone of genius, too. Knowing which tasks you enjoy doing the most and are the best at will help give you some clues early on about how to grow your business.

Too many different kinds of tasks can lead to VA overwhelm and client frustration because your clients expect the same level of quality across the board. Imagine how hard it'd be to balance all of these different tasks as a virtual assistant if your primary focus was building a YouTube following and channel: Email marketing, repurposing podcast episodes into blogs, completing personal travel research, buying gifts for employees and high-end clients, and uploading blog posts into the WordPress platform.

For these common reasons, many virtual assistants put together retainer proposals or packages. This allows them to define the type of tasks they want to work on. For example, I've partnered with a Pinterest virtual assistant in the past. All she does is maximize my Pinterest strategy and provide me with monthly reports. If I were to ask her to take on building my Twitter following, that might not be too far outside her zone of genius as she is a social media expert. But she has learned the best way to be an expert in her field and to be efficient with her time is to focus on one social media channel alone.

You don't have to commit to this at the outset of your virtual assistant business, but it's something to keep in mind if you encounter a client asking you to complete 25 different tasks and step in with expertise at a high level on all of them.

# 5
# SERVICES TO OFFER AS A VA

WHEN YOU'RE FIRST getting started as a virtual assistant, you can take one of the most important steps to narrow down what services you'll provide to clients. Some virtual assistants choose to take a jack-of-all-trades approach, which can certainly be one way to get your foot in the door and learn which services you do and don't like.

However, this can also make it feel like you're juggling 20 balls at any given time and can make for a very confusing experience going forward. That's why it's recommended that you think carefully about the services you choose to provide.

To succeed as a virtual assistant and set up a package to offer to your clients, you need to know your skills. This is the key question for a new VA: what services should I offer and which ones should I avoid? This varies greatly based on your comfort level with various services, but I'm going to give you some ideas for how to determine what you're best at and also things you're familiar or not familiar with.

You'll be spending a good portion of your day working on projects for clients. You want to feel confident that you're interested enough in these subjects and services to speak about them during sales calls. You don't want to get bored or overwhelmed in trying to focus on what you've decided to offer.

The perfect combination of virtual assistant services is something you enjoy doing, something that pays well, and something in high demand. When all of these factors align, it's the perfect opportunity for you.

When stumped on what services to offer, please check out the handout PDF at www.virtualassistantbook.com that guides you through what many popular kinds of VAs do, how they do it, and what they charge. This is a great way to get inspiration for the kinds of things you could choose to offer. You might already have some things in the back of your mind that might be a good fit based on your past experience or level of interest.

## Determine Your Starting Point

It can be both a good and bad thing that there are so many kinds of tasks a virtual assistant can do. Though it makes for a lot of variety and helps protect the market from getting too saturated with VAs, it also can make it harder for new VAs to know which skills to offer.

Keep this in mind: do *not* select a service or skill because you heard it was in high demand or paid well. If you do that service four to eight hours a day and hate it, you'll burn out quickly and even close up shop. Just because there's possible money in something doesn't mean you should do it. However, many VAs might have otherwise had a great start to their business.

Here are a few questions to help you get started as you work through this chapter and decide what you want to offer:

- What past experience do you have doing certain services?

- What did you love about your last job?

- Is there something you've always wanted to learn but haven't been able to due to other commitments?

## What Services to Avoid?

It's also important to think about what services you shouldn't offer. This is a great debate in the industry because a lot of times you'll have clients who'll hire you to do one thing, and then you'll evolve into doing different roles for them. But it's important to keep in mind that you don't always have to accept a new task or opportunity presented by your client. If it's something you're uncomfortable with, it's up to you to say no.

And one of the reasons why it's not a good idea to take on work you're not passionate about is because even if it pays very well, it'll only end up costing you in terms of headaches. You're less likely to deliver higher quality, and it'll more likely take longer for you to complete the project. If you're billing hourly, the client can get frustrated by that. On the flip side, work that you love to do inspires you and increases your client's commitment to working with you because it's really easy to see somebody's passion come through when working on a project they care about. But it's also easy to see their frustration if they're working on something they don't care about. If you want to learn more about your skills, I recommend two things to help you identify some outstanding virtual assistant jobs and clients. So, combined with the stoplight list you made of tasks you put together, knowing your skills through something like a Meyers-Briggs or the Fascinator test can be wonderful for confirming that a job you're considering is the right fit for you. And this completes the first video of module two.

As a new virtual assistant, you might not yet have the experience or interest in pursuing a particular type of work as a VA. Rest assured that you can get initial experience doing an internship, take on small projects, and work with people early on to get feedback and grow your testimonials list. You might take on a broad variety of projects and tasks to discover what you like and get some experience in navigating common tools.

## Look for Something You like Doing

Simply put, if you aren't engaged with your virtual assistant business by doing work that inspires or interests you, there's a good chance you'll get sick of it and burn out. You might also miss deadlines with your clients, making them unhappy as well. Even if something seems interesting initially, it's not uncommon to discover that you don't like particular services.

As you get more experience as a VA, you'll feel more confident in changing your services. So, don't be afraid of this most important step first. If you hate working on technical tasks, you should never attempt to learn Keap or educate yourself as a Keap expert. While this is a lucrative service to offer as a virtual assistant, it can be a major headache if you're not passionate about those technical tasks.

## Look for Tasks That Pay Well

Basic data entry is probably the simplest form of virtual assistant work and often comes at a lower hourly rate. Many virtual assistants also choose to package this in with their general hourly rate. More advanced services like managing team members or managing complex software applications, however, command a higher hourly rate or a higher project rate than other types of projects.

You'll probably try a little bit of everything beginning with your passion and confidence when you get started. If you're brand new to working online, you probably wouldn't launch your VA business with email marketing services. You might start out with data entry, calendar support, or web research. As you learn more and get more experience, you might branch out to new service offerings. Start with where you have the most comfort level or level of interest.

The best thing you can do after you've identified services you like to complete is determining what the paying market is like. To get a sense of this, you can simply post a job on any popular online job board sites like:

- Freelancer

- Guru

- Upwork

These sites give a general idea of what other people in the marketplace would charge for these particular services—type in things like "virtual assistant "to start with a general search. Then, narrow down the search by adding other terms based on the services you're interested in. If you don't see anyone posting jobs for that skillset, it might not be in enough demand for you to make consistent income.

## Make Sure There Is a Market Demand for That Service

It's great to be an expert at working in Excel, for example, but what if there's no one out there who wants to hire a virtual assistant to help him or her with Excel? You can do your market research for this category by expanding on what you just did on the freelance job board site by posting a request for proposals and evaluating the response.

Online job board sites can be a general indicator of whether or not there is demand in the marketplace for the type of service you're thinking about offering. Spend some time evaluating the administrative support or virtual assistant section of these online marketplaces to determine how many job posts request the types of service you're interested in. The work that people are already looking for help with is a great way to tell whether you're in line with current client demand.

Virtual assistance has become much more of a broad term and now covers a variety of tasks. Virtual assistant services involve artistic skills, computing skills, management, editing, research, and more. And if you're skilled in a particular area or enjoy creating certain business elements, why not charge for that service and have a job that makes you happy while generating a regular income? There are many tasks you probably perform regularly and don't realize you could make money from them! Sometimes there are tasks others consider mundane but are simple for others. In these situations, a VAs skillset makes them employable and optimizable.

Here are twenty examples of *mundane* tasks largely sought after by business owners:

1. Newsletter design

2. Newsletter management

3. Email reminders

4. Newsletter content creation

5. Email automation

6. Branding services

7. Press releases

8. Market research

9. Travel research and booking

10. Affiliate management

11. Web assistant

12. Photoshop / Illustrator assistance

13. Social media assistance

14. Social media advertisement creation/set-up

15. Content creation services

16. Technical writing and tutorials

17. Landing page creation

18. WordPress services

19. Graphic design – logo and web

20. eBook content and design

No matter your skill set, whether you have an eye for artistic elements, or you're a resourceful manager, the business elements you thrive at creating can be turned into a career. If you have a skill or talent you enjoy doing, outsource that skill as a virtual assistant. Then, earn money while doing what you love.

Increasingly, there are more virtual assistants to compete with in the marketplace. There's a big interest in working from home, and since virtual assisting has a pretty low barrier to entry, if you've got the right skills and personality traits, there are more VAs every day! As a result, what used to work well in the marketplace as far as offering many different services for your possible clients doesn't always allow you to stand out.

Imagine this scenario that I spot four or five times a week in "Facebook groups": Someone posts a job lead that they "need a VA "or "need admin help."(Zero points for writing a great job description, but yet these posts show up all the time.) Inevitably, up to 50 people respond to this post sharing a mini-pitch or a link to their website.

Let me introduce you to an advanced freelancing concept. When clients are overloaded with pitches from people seemingly no different from one another, they choose no one at all or the first person who responded. You'll also see more posts in places like Upwork and "Facebook groups" asking for someone specific:

- Give me your best recommendations for a Pinterest strategist

- Anyone know a VA who is a rockstar with Active Campaign?

- Who has worked with an excellent VA for publishing blogs on WordPress?

These asks highlight great thinking on the part of the person posting them; they're looking for something very specific from a person who more than likely has a niche or area of focus in that area.

When you first start working as a VA, you might not know which software you like or how much variety you want to have in your day. That's okay—it's perfectly normal to spend some time as a generalist (i.e., the VA who offers 20 different services) before narrowing down.

If you decide to offer specialized services in the future, you don't have to limit yourself to one thing. You can always choose a handful of services where you maintain your knowledge to have a nice variety. Perhaps you like email marketing and graphic design, and sometimes, there'll be a crossover with those two services. It's reasonable that you could stay up to speed on all the latest trends in both.

## Niching as a Virtual Assistant

I want to bring up two important concepts as you think more about structuring your services as a VA. The first is why it's in your best interest to niche, and the second is the two different ways you can niche as a virtual assistant.

You might think you could make more money offering everything, right? If you offer yourself up as a comprehensive virtual assistant who can do everything, then you'll get the opportunity to work with more clients and to make more money. However, the reality is that it's tough to find a virtual assistant who is an expert at everything. Some entrepreneurs hiring their first VA think there is such a thing as the mythical VA who can do it all. But it's very hard to identify someone who fulfills that role.

Everyone has different strengths and different interests. This is why it makes sense to focus in a niche where you can serve your clients in a meaningful way rather than offering yourself as a jack of all trades. It's better to say there are some things I'm good at and some things I'm not so good at. You could let down your clients, so why not focus on what you do best, and deliver that in an incredible way for your clients, so they're happy and refer you to others.

There may be several services you offer within your niche, but I don't recommend doing everything because you're likely to find you don't enjoy that. Plus, you might not be strong at every kind of task or working at every kind of industry.

So, if that's not your skillset to jump around social media, data entry, editing, and posting, why not choose to focus on doing something particular for clients like specializing on social media only?

Then, you're spending three to four hours a day working on somebody's social media strategy and can become a social media expert and get to know their brand and their voice very well, which benefits you and the client.

When you have so many responsibilities on your plate, and you're an expert in some and a newbie in others, it's easy to drop the ball, procrastinate, and push off tasks you don't like or understand. That's when you're more likely to work on those tasks you naturally gravitate toward and are good at. So, you may ask how you'll know your niche. The best time to discover your niche is as early on as possible but you need some experience.

Take on a couple of test contracts that aren't full-time engagements and not excessive amounts of work. It'll allow you a chance to try your hand at something committed to the client long term.

That goes with any job. Get some experience. Pick three to five things you think you might be interested in doing and try a trial job with someone. Work for a few hours and get your feet wet. That'll help begin to guide you in the direction of your niche.

Specializing means you get deeper and deeper with your level of focus and expertise, which lends future credibility when it's time to raise your rates. It makes it easy for your current clients to refer you to someone else, but it also makes it easier for you to bring on new clients too. Commanding higher rates is something you want to work toward, so it's hard to break out of a rate rut if you're offering services across the board and jumping from one thing to another.

As you go through this process, the right niche should emerge. Even if you're starting as a generalist, a jack of all trades, or don't know what you want to do yet, certain things will appeal to you. As you gain more experience and work for your first couple of clients, other tasks that take longer will drive you crazy and aggravate you. Keep a note of both.

Let me give you an actual example. I love posting things for my clients, because when it's on a website platform I can easily understand, I know I can do it quickly and correctly. However, if someone comes to me with a technology problem, that's not my area of expertise. I'm upfront about my lack of technological skills.

Let's recap the most important lessons here. What's a niche? It's something you choose to specialize in. It could be a type of task, a particular kind of client, or an industry. Maybe you provide services only to life coaches or personal trainers. Why should you niche? It allows you to become an expert, serve the client effectively and efficiently, and continue that marketing vehicle because clients love giving you more work or referring business your way.

## Filling the Skills Gap

If you're relatively new to the world of working online, you might take a look at your resume and realize you've been out of the workforce for a while or not up to speed with the latest trends in social media, project management, or email management. Once you identify a skills gap, this doesn't mean you should hang up your plan of working as a virtual assistant. It's quite the opposite. Now that you know where you might have some room to improve, you can use this information to help you get up to speed.

You don't necessarily need a paid project to show that you can exercise a certain skill. Your willingness to learn will often allow you to overcome some of the challenges and show the client you have serious passion and drive about becoming a virtual assistant.

Thanks to how much content exists online today, there are plenty of options to fill your skills gap. Start with free tools like podcasts and YouTube tutorials. A great next place to expand your skillset is Udemy.com. There, you'll be able to download ebooks and enroll in online courses specific to what you'd like to learn next. For those interested in digital marketing, HubSpot also offers free courses and certifications on things like email marketing and social media. Check out the last chapter of this book to get a full list and links to free and paid trainings for some of the most popular software programs and skills for VAs!

# 6
# CLIENT QUALIFICATION AND MANAGEMENT FOR VAS

WHO DO YOU want to work with?

If you're a new VA, I bet your answer is "with anyone who wants to pay me!"

While I understand that sentiment, it's off base. Not everyone should be your client and want to work with you. And didn't you want to start your business, so you have some say over who you work with, anyway?

This is something no one ever told me when I started doing admin work online for a real estate agent—you have the flexibility to decline work because someone is difficult, gives bad directions, or doesn't respect your boundaries.

But beyond some of the obvious red flags for clients you wouldn't want to work with, you also get to decide if you want to narrow your focus in terms of who you work with.

As a publicist today, I love working with people whose missions I can get behind. I work with inspiring and committed professionals trying to bring a great message to the world. Working with them not only generates money for my business and experience for me, but I truly love helping further their cause.

And you might have a passion for something in the virtual assisting world too! Maybe you've always thought about starting a blog but would rather help someone else with a known brand run and manage their blog. Perhaps you love Pinterest as a personal user and want to see how coaches and small business owners leverage it.

The concept of working for an ideal client is simple, but it's one you might not have ever been introduced to in real life—you get to decide who you want to work with. Those characteristics can be as broad (people paying you on time) or as narrow (military spouse entrepreneurs running online businesses as bloggers or course creators) as you want.

When I graduated from my master's program, it was in the midst of the 2008 recession. It was an awful time to leave school and look for employment, even with a master's degree. After several months of searching, I answered phones at an insurance agency and scanned paperwork to carriers. One thing I hated about that job was the idea that the customer was always right. We worked with a lot of life insurance agents who were not always right. Sometimes, they were rude, condescending, or downright harassing. But I had to sit there, smile, and take it no matter what they dished out, even when it wasn't even remotely my fault.

Some people are plain difficult. And that's fine. But when I launched my business, I made my first commitment to myself: I'm not working with anyone like that. It means that I've ended sales calls because the person cursed at their in-office support when they forgot to put me on hold. I've declined chances to work with people who acted like I was stupid or not qualified enough. These are things I would've never gotten away with in my insurance desk job. We would've been told to make the insurance agent happy no matter how miserable they made us or how little money they brought in.

Being a business owner was a game-changer. And working with only ideal clients (and screening out those I missed at first glance) kept me excited about my business and able to deliver a top-notch experience to those I do work with. Win-win.

## Determining Your Ideal Client as a VA

Do you remember the thrill of landing your first client? Even if you haven't yet landed a virtual assistant client, you're probably very excited about the opportunity of working for somebody and being paid for your skill in a virtual capacity.

In these early stages, you must be aware of the potential downfalls of bringing on every client who offers you a position. While most people who want to hire virtual assistants are reputable and quality clients, there are plenty of scams and red flags to be mindful of when first starting out. The more experience you get working as a virtual assistant, the easier it'll be to tell when you're working with an ideal client.

It's challenging to niche down as a virtual assistant and decide exactly who your ideal client is when you're brand-new to the marketplace and haven't had the opportunity to work with a variety of clients. Even though you'll gain this experience over time and decipher who your ideal clients are, knowing about this in advance can help you to identify these people when you come upon them and the red flags that could and should block you from working with others.

Unfortunately, I've known dozens of virtual assistants who've been badly burned by partnering with the wrong client. These can be things like not getting paid, being asked to work all hours of the day or night, and being berated because instructions weren't provided and accurately. Virtual assistants must be prepared to protect themselves and respond appropriately using contracts, screening calls and test jobs, and communication skills to navigate some of these challenges if and when they emerge with clients.

Even though I've gone into some detail here about some of the downsides of working with bad clients, there are plenty of valuable and ideal clients. These can be some of the most exciting people to work for because they make it so easy to provide services and skills you're already passionate about. These are your ideal clients.

Some of the following traits might represent ideal clients for you:

- provides clear instructions

- pays your invoices on time

- provides you with bonuses or extra learning opportunities

- communicates with you professionally during your established business hours

- says "thank you"

- refers you to other clients

- provides you with testimonials to help you land future work

Simply put, ideal clients are the people you're excited to work for and hope to have a long-term relationship with. These are the clients who are truly a joy to interact with and make you excited each day to complete your work as a virtual assistant.

The above examples are likely universal qualities VAs look for. You might also have particular personality characteristics in mine. For example, when I began my virtual assistant business, I spent a lot of time on the phone with prospective clients. While this was a good opportunity to meet with them and decide whether or not we were fit, it also set the precedent that I'd be available by phone to answer questions, which I should receive compensation for. Instead, it led to problems down the road when I worked via calls but didn't get paid for that time.

Shortly thereafter, I updated my ideal client screening questions to determine how much phone time would be required to network with my clients. I also updated all of my contracts to ensure that I'd be paid for additional time spent on the phone above and beyond anything else we'd agreed to as part of a kick-off package. This meant that I tended to repel those clients who wanted me to spend a lot of time on the phone or expected me to do this on an unpaid basis. Simultaneously, I attracted clients who provided clear and compelling instructions upfront that allowed me to do what I needed to do without regular check-in calls.

Defining an ideal client might also involve plenty of experience in working with prospective clients to narrow down the type of industry or type of projects on which you prefer to work. For example, you might find that you have a particular interest in email marketing and therefore tailor your future virtual assistant offerings to focus only on email management and marketing. You can also combine various services and become known as a social media manager and an email marketing manager. The good news is that you don't have to make this decision now, and there are plenty of virtual assistants who specialize in particular Industries, software, or projects. And those who do a broad variety of tasks enjoy learning and doing something different every day.

## Red Flags for VA Clients

Since you won't know who your ideal client is until you have had some opportunity to work with different people, it's easier to explain some of the red flags you should be mindful of while beginning to market your business. Not all of these red flags will necessarily be folded into your business. Still, they can help to know the personality types you intend to avoid or limit your interactions with in the future.

## The Blamer

In initial calls with your clients, it's helpful to ask if they have experience working with a virtual assistant. It isn't uncommon for some clients to have attempted outsourcing before. Some of these clients have been successful with their efforts, and others will be frustrated. What's important to know here is whether the client places all of the blame on the virtual assistant or feels multiple VAs weren't up to the task. When a client has partnered with five or more virtual assistants and has been unsuccessful with a project, it's likely a problem with the client rather than the virtual assistant. Listen carefully to the words used by your client on your intake call to see if they regularly blame other people when the client might have had some level of responsibility for the fall out in the project.

## The Disorganized Client

I'm a disorganized client when I outsource to my virtual assistants. (Might as well be honest, right?) I recognize this can be a real challenge for some people. Others thrive on working with me to fix it.

With multiple balls in the air, it can be challenging for some clients to provide you with daily check-ins. Many of the virtual assistants who work on my team are self-directed and independent workers. This means that unless they hit a snag or an obstacle such as being unable to get inside a software program, they'll work alone until the project reaches the point that they need my review. This works well for my team, but you might be the type of virtual assistant who needs regular check-ins and more organization. During your interview with prospective clients, ask about their communication style and some of the current challenges in their business. If you're a highly organized person, it might be the perfect project for you to step in and help organize some of their files, strategies, tools, and plans.

## The Negotiator Client

If the first words out of the prospective client's mouth are about offering a discount on your virtual assistant services, you might be in for a long ride of having to prove your worth continually.

A client who offers you something in exchange for discounted prices might be able to negotiate down your rates. But if that's the only thing the client seems to care about is paying a cheaper rate or comparing you to other virtual assistants who've quoted a less-expensive rate, it can be an uphill battle for you to prove that you've logged the hours you claim and are worth this higher rate. This doesn't come down to an actual statement of your worth regarding your rate but rather the client's perception of what they're willing to pay.

## The Hard to Reach Client

If you're working on a project that requires a lot of feedback or insight from your client, it can be challenging to work with someone constantly on-the-go or who works strange hours. For example, suppose you're helping to build out a website for your client but don't receive feedback on the brand, colors, and style. In that case, it can be very difficult to get this information reviewed if you're working in completely opposite time zones or if your client regularly skips out on showing up to phone calls. Thankfully, you can use tools like Voxer to stay in touch and get quick feedback.

Sometimes, it's more effective to reach out to clients with these quick little voice messages or comments in a program like Slack so that you can get a simple response without having to worry about getting on your client's busy calendar. But if your client is never around and is simply hard to reach, you'll find yourself stuck and hitting obstacles at numerous points in the process. If you're the type of person who likes to see projects completed from beginning to end, the fact that it's hard to get a hold of your client can be very challenging.

# How to Stand Out for Your Ideal Clients

The more you can do to know who your ideal client is (and isn't), the easier it'll be to attract the right people to work with you. Here are some tips on how to make that happen.

## Go Above and Beyond

A good way to make a great first impression is to go a little above and beyond what's expected.

This doesn't mean you have to provide hours and hours of work beyond what your pay or work for ten hours of free work before the client hires you. But think about the next step you could accomplish in a project or think about questions they might have after reviewing your work. Doing this simple step shows that you care and are committed to their business. One of my first VAs really stood out to me because she looked at my website and had some specific questions about what I did. It showed me that she'd done more than surface-level prep.

## Do the Research

Make sure you research each project. If the instructions aren't clear or you don't feel like you have everything you need to accomplish something, it's better to know that upfront and then tell your client, "Hey, I am missing pieces here, and I need some more details." It's way better to acknowledge this at the beginning of a project than when the client is expecting you to turn in completed work, and you haven't started because of a stumbling block.

## Deliver What You Say You Will

This sounds obvious, but it needs to be said. Deliver what you say you will, and that puts you in the driver's seat, because if a client asks you when you can complete something, this simply means you need to be honest about a completion date. You can explain to them some of the limitations on your side and how the schedule may work for you, but stick true to what you say you're going to deliver. If you say you're going to do something in a week and it's the sixth day, but now you're emailing the client for further instructions, that shows you haven't really taken this seriously. Deliver what you say you will, and if you can't do it, share that.

Make sure you complete project goals with their business in mind, not yours. This means that you're thinking about what their company could use or what their life could use if you're a virtual assistant. What are their business goals?

Think about who they're working with: Who are their clients? What are the challenges your client faces? Whatever you do to address this can be really helpful, and the client will instantly see you as a major asset because you're thinking about their bottom line and their end goals rather than yours. It's really hard to part ways with a VA who you feel is so committed to your company because it builds that trust and loyalty.

Remember that it's not about completing a project as quickly as possible. If you're working on something where you're being paid by project, it's very tempting to think about wrapping it up quickly to get paid. But if you miss things or show sloppy work, the client isn't going to want to work with you beyond this project. They might even terminate an ongoing business relationship. So, it's not about completing things as quickly as possible. It's about doing them correctly.

## Stay One Step Ahead

Being one step ahead of your client shows that you're committed to their business and their success. I can't recommend this strongly enough. Think about the challenges your client might be facing.

For example, if you got a task from your client that said, "I need help determining what email marketing program to use," you could conduct the research and put together a spreadsheet. But think about what questions they'd still have, and perhaps point them to additional articles for the top one or two pieces of software you recommend. This is a great way to anticipate their concerns and be one step ahead of what they need. It also helps to cement long-term relationships.

## Be Honest When You Can't Meet a Deadline

If you fall behind for one reason or another, be honest.

Just communicate if you're going to miss a deadline. If you notice that the time to turn something in is drawing near and you aren't going to be done, send them a message. If something personal happens in your life, and it's going to hold you back from completing the task, let them know. I'd always rather know that something is going on rather than expect something and realize that you've dropped off the face of the earth. I think this is true of most clients that you're going to work with as a virtual assistant.

Approach everything with a neutral tone and suggest what you could do better in the future and what the client could do to help you. When you frame solving problems in the perception that this will make your client's life and business easier, they're going to be more receptive to hearing it, especially if you're saying what you think you could do better as well.

## Ask for Better Instructions When You Need Them

If you don't have the right amount of instructions from your client, don't be afraid to ask for help. Sometimes, instructions are the biggest issue in a relationship between a VA and a client because the instructions are unclear or not written well. I give specific instructions to my virtual assistants and all of my entrepreneurs I work with in the hiring process.

A VA can feel stupid and unmotivated if the instructions are unclear. Where there is room for improvement there, tell the client how you prefer to receive instruction. Do screen capture videos help? Do you need written instructions? Do you need to walk through this with them as they do it? Make sure you provide the opportunity to make this a learning experience for both of you, and don't be afraid to ask. Again, it's better to get additional information so that you can turn something in right the first time.

## Be Upfront When Something Is Impossible

If a project seems impossible, share your concerns with the client. Don't be afraid to say, "I'm sorry. I need more information here," or "I've attempted to start phase one of this project, but it looks like it's not going to be possible." You'll notice that a lot of these themes keep coming back to communication. Keeping that line of communication open goes a long way.

When you share concerns about a project that seems overly difficult or even impossible, explain why and tell your client how you came to your conclusion. More often than not, they'll be happy that you took the time to be honest about it and try to come up with another task or another way of approaching this issue.

Part of the reason for talking about impossible projects is that your client needs to know limits. When you first hire a virtual assistant and give them ten tasks and they succeed at all of them, it's very easy to fall into the trap as a client of thinking this VA can do everything without limits.

Every so often, though, you'll receive a task, or your client will give you a task that doesn't make a lot of sense, and you can't complete it. Then, you'll be really stuck when you can't do what was asked of you. Your client needs to know your limits. And again, if this is something where you require additional information or education, suggest how the two of you could accomplish that together. Some of these limitations can be broken down.

For example, if you were given a task to do some HTML coding and only have basic skills in that area, you might want to learn more. Perhaps you could suggest an online course to take that'd educate you more on this subject matter. In this situation, if the client intends to use you on this task regularly, he/she should pay for it. This allows you to show your client that you want to continue growing and learning.

That being said, if you hate HTML coding, and it's really not in your wheelhouse, then point out it's not really what you do. When it's something you don't enjoy or something likely to frustrate you, your client needs to know this.

My final thought is that success is all about consistency when you're working with virtual assistant clients. Be in open communication with your clients. Share concerns when they emerge, point out what you can do better, make sure you always have crystal clear instructions and be one step ahead of your client. If you implement these thoughts into your practices as a virtual assistant today, there is no doubt that you'll be working with some amazing and thrilled clients over the long haul.

# 7
# FINDING CLIENTS AND MARKETING

THE OPPORTUNITY TO become a VA has never been hotter. But that means it's more important than ever to stand out from the crowd. In this chapter, you'll learn more about why you need to market and some ideas and tips to get you started.

Marketing requires you to put yourself out there and have a multi-pronged approach to finding and connecting with potential clients.

Casting a wide net is key for getting enough pitches and connections. You can't send one pitch a week and hope to get results. You need to post at least ten pitches per week minimum (including all the different forms of your marketing, like connecting directly with people on LinkedIn or responding to an Upwork post) to have enough conversations.

When you're working in a competitive market like virtual assistance, you have to be a unicorn in a field of horses. You have to jump out as both the person qualified to do the tasks and the most qualified given their unique situation.

To build up your business, you'll need to be very proactive with your marketing. There are two kinds of marketing virtual assistants can use: direct marketing to clients and indirect marketing. In direct marketing, you're reaching out to or responding directly to prospective clients: sending pitches on Upwork, connecting on LinkedIn, or scanning other job boards. Indirect marketing includes posting on social media, writing blogs, and spend time doing things like optimizing your LinkedIn profile.

## Creating a Marketing Plan for Your Virtual Assistant Business

When you don't have any clients at the beginning of your business, you'll dedicate most of your time to marketing as mentioned previously. Determine the amount of time you have available to work on your virtual assistant business and break that down into how you'll divvy it up over the week.

Since at least 80% of your time will be spent branding yourself, networking, and putting yourself out there, you should have a streamlined or targeted plan to make this happen. For example, in a given week for somebody who has ten hours to dedicate to building their virtual assistant business, that could include the following:

- One hour per day scanning Upwork.

- A 20-minute check each night on relevant job boards, including Flex Jobs and Remote.co

- Two hours' worth of time developing content marketing, such as blog posts, LinkedIn shares, or material to be posted on your website.

- Time spent individually reaching out to solopreneurs and small business owners on LinkedIn to leverage your connection requests.

- Time spent networking in "Facebook groups" where jobs for virtual assistants are posted.

Brand new freelancers often ask how much time they should spend pitching. The answer varies based on the overall amount of time you have to give and your goals for your virtual assistant business. Still, the truth is if you're only sending one or two pitches per week or spending an hour every single week marketing, you're simply not doing enough work to generate clients. I refer to this as the client funnel.

Clients at every stage of the process will drop off, so you need to have enough marketing done to generate a lot of conversations at the top of the funnel. You should spend at least several hours per week on marketing efforts. As you grow in your virtual assistant business, you'll learn more about your most successful marketing methods. Over time, you can release the marketing methods that don't lead to conversions for you and focus primarily on your top two or three ways of growing your virtual assistant business.

However, when you start, it's helpful to have four or five marketing methods you're essentially testing to see how well they perform for you. It isn't uncommon to get a lot of no's when you first start out. You're still fine-tuning your branding, pitching, and the unique value proposition you present to clients. So, it's completely normal but every conversation won't result in a client. Even though virtual assistant work is much easier to break into than other freelancing types where you'd need to showcase specific skills like graphic design or web development, this is a very competitive market, and clients have a lot of choices. This means you must do your due diligence in presenting what is unique about you and the process you bring to the table.

## Reviewing Your Resume and Pulling Out Your Unique Value Proposition

In this section, I'm going to walk you through an exercise I typically do with the candidates in my Operation Freelance Non-Profit, where I train military spouses and veterans how to break into freelancing. Aside from the skills you bring to the table or skills you've taken time to pick up and learn, there are other ways to pull from your existing resume and background to determine your unique value proposition.

You can also use one of the most common questions asked in part-time and full-time job interviews to help present yourself successfully to potential clients as a virtual assistant: If I were to ask a past manager or supervisor what they'd say about you, what words would they use to describe your work performance? The bottom line is that any virtual assistant should be able to complete tasks. This means that when a client is looking at 20 different virtual assistants, price alone shouldn't be the only differentiating point between all those VAs. Confused and over-whelmed clients don't buy.

It's your responsibility to pull out what is unique about you and present this to clients in a meaningful way. This is known as your unique value proposition. For example, imagine that one of your past managers or supervisors says you're an excellent team player. This is very important to repurpose into a conversation around virtual assistant work because even if you might not nec-essarily be working with a big team, it shows prospective clients that you're willing to put the client and company's needs first. That's a precious skill for a virtual assistant to have and one that you can bring up in your website copy, in your marketing, in your initial pitches, and conversations with clients.

If a past supervisor appreciated that you never missed a dead-line, highlight that. It might be the one thing that jumps out about your application when a client considers multiple candi-dates. Your content marketing's overall goal and the materials you put out about yourself are to convince the client that you're the right person for the job.

Psychologically, this means you should transition into thinking about what it'd be like to work with you before they even hire you. I can't tell you how many times clients have pulled out specific lines from my pitches, LinkedIn posts, or blog posts that made them decide to reach out. Perhaps it was the direct words of another client that I used to share a testimonial or how easy I made it seem to work with me. All of these are unique differentiating points and are very valuable for bringing up to your prospective clients.

# Seven Popular Ways to Market Your Freelance VA Business

## 1. Upwork

Upwork is usually the first place someone hunting for a VA will go, so it's good to have a profile there. Upwork **is an online marketplace** where contractors and clients connect, and it can be a great source of ongoing work too! If you're not fond of Upwork, other sites like it can be used, including Guru or Freelancer.

## 2. Facebook groups

Find "Facebook groups" where entrepreneurs hang out and network there. As entrepreneurs post questions, you can provide free value and cement yourself as a knowledgeable service provider. Many of these groups have weekly posts where individuals ask for help or referrals. Being active and answering other people's questions are a great way to show your value.

## 3. Following prominent entrepreneurs

People who run successful online companies are already far more likely to hire a virtual assistant, and it's unlikely you'll have to pitch them on the overall value of a VA. There are plenty of successful Internet gurus, but here are a couple I recommend following. Sign up for their email list so you can get first wind of opportunities:

- Jeff Walker

- Lisa Sasevich

- Justin Livingston/Callan Rush

- Amy Porterfield

- Brendan Burchard

If you follow these leaders, you'll likely see who their peers are too! They often promote one another's products and interact in that way so that you can use this to snowball!

## 4. Pinterest

If you're an avid social media user, having an amazing Pinterest account shows your value to clients. Consider creating your content about how a VA can help your business. Promoting this shows that you're a professional and helps sell clients on your value before they plan to hire you!

## 5. LinkedIn

If there's a social media platform where most professionals hang out, it's LinkedIn. Publishing valuable content even once a week about how virtual assistants can transform your business works well!

## 6. Your own website/email list

Offering a free report that helps entrepreneurs be more effective with their time can weave in a lot of valuable information about hiring a VA. Put them into an automatic email sequence where they get a free 20-minute call with you to talk about how you can help. After getting to know you through a free report and your email sequence, they already trust you.

As a new VA, you may feel overwhelmed, and that's normal. If you're feeling like you can't handle marketing all these simultaneously, that's okay. Pick one or two to focus on. As you fine-tune your process and enhance your skills, you'll either have so much work from the first sites you selected you won't need to do any more marketing, or you can branch out into other methods.

7. Other job boards. Places like FlexJobs and Remote.co are other places to scope our virtual assistant opportunities. I like to scan these a couple of times a week to see if anything interested has been posted.

## Why Private Clients Benefit You

Before we start, let's define what a private client is. Many people use popular online job board sites like Guru, Freelancer, and Upwork to initiate their freelance career as a virtual assistant. Over time, you'll ultimately want to enroll people you choose to work with directly. This means that the client has been passed to you through a referral, or you've somehow connected with them, or they're pursuing you outside of a job board service.

Even if you hope to look at jobs on Upwork regularly, you'll still want to include some aspect of seeking out private clients. Making yourself available to multiple sources of clients only helps you grow your business.

## Job Board Clients vs. Private Clients

Clients from job boards can be a beneficial way to build your freelance virtual assistant career, but you ultimately don't want to stay there together. Part of the reason for this is they're always going to take a cut of your income. Freelance sites like Upwork take 10% to 20% of your income and will go down to 5% if you've been working with that client a lot and earned more than $10,000.

But if you can bring this client in on your own, you have more say over the payment terms, and you're not paying a middleman to facilitate the process of your business relationship. So, ongoing projects with clients you've elected to work with outside of any intermediary or third party are a great way to build your business. It'll also allow you to be in control of all of the terms of your working relationship.

## How Private VA Clients Benefit Your Business

Private VA clients benefit your business in numerous ways. When you work directly with a private client, you become an expert on their needs. You'll learn their business, preferred style, how they like to do business, and how they like to communicate. When you're well-liked, you're more hirable and susceptible to raises when appropriate.

Sometimes, the online job board atmosphere means that clients are tempted to believe they can go back and find somebody else because employees are easily replaceable. If they're unhappy with a particular virtual assistant or freelancer, they can hire somebody else.

When you've taken the time to form that private relationship with someone and deliver amazing value, they're much more likely to hire you for ongoing work and give you raises as your job role changes and becomes more important in their company.

Private clients get to know you as opposed to the middleman. The client gets to know how you work as a virtual assistant, they get to know your strengths and weaknesses, and they're more committed to building a long-term relationship.

Ultimately, these long-term, ongoing relationships between you and your freelance virtual assistant clients can allow you to have more confidence over your monthly income, and it will enable you to become more and more of an expert on their business. This leads to a happier working relationship overall.

Private clients also are more likely to offer you ongoing work, meaning you can spend less time marketing. This is why it's so important that you form a solid relationship with the client as soon as you have the opportunity to work together. Show how dedicated you are to this client's goals to indicate your value to that client early on. Most people in need of a virtual assistant don't need a virtual assistant to work on only one project. Rather, they need someone in their business regularly contributing to projects, tasks, and ideas.

# Finding VA Clients on Upwork

If you're just getting started as a virtual assistant, it might seem overwhelming to try and land business on your own. It can feel unnatural to try cold calling. Perhaps you're not quite sure who your ideal client is, but you want to be able to work for someone online. The barriers involved with setting up a website, getting your feet wet, and bringing on your first client can feel overwhelming.

Some people are ready to hit the ground running with a new career as a virtual assistant until they realize it's just too much to handle at once. This is why I strongly recommend that a brand new VA consider finding virtual assistant work on Upwork. Upwork is one of the most popular online job board sites out there today.

## Basics of Landing Virtual Assistant Work on Upwork

Here's how it works.

A client visits Upwork and posts a request for proposals. In this process, he or she outlines various aspects of the job:

- What the job entails
- How many hours per week or month to expect to work

- The ideal qualities of the right applicant

- What to provide to be considered

## Types of Virtual Assistant Contracts on Upwork

You'll find two major groups of clients on Upwork looking for a VA: someone who needs help with a short-term project, and someone looking to hire a long-term VA. Depending on where you're at with your business, one may make more sense for you than the other. Ultimately, a great way to build your VA business is to hire someone you can regularly work with. This is because you build a relationship and cut down on the marketing work you have to do to fill your schedule.

There are two major reasons why I recommend you start your career by finding virtual assistant work on Upwork: the clients are presold, and the process allows you to get started with much less legwork.

As I shared above, it can be time-consuming or frustrating to take all the steps to start a virtual assistant business. Maybe you're not even sure yet whether you want to own a VA business. Upwork enables you to give it a shot and decide for yourself.

Since a client on Upwork already knows that they want help, you have one less barrier to getting started. The client knows they want to hire someone and are looking for the right person.

That's where you come in. On Upwork, it's your job to convince the client that you're the best person. You do this by bidding on the job and showing your interest and background. If the client is interested, they may hire you directly on the site or reach out to you for more information.

You can sign up for a free Upwork account today and start your profile set up. Your profile and pitch to clients are the most important elements involve in landing virtual assistant work on Upwork. You can spend an hour or two putting this together and be ready to bid on jobs.

When you're getting started, it's natural that you'll need to make things as easy as possible for yourself. Putting yourself out there as a business owner can be nerve-wracking, even when you're otherwise confident in various aspects of your life.

Upwork makes things easy because you can see whether you need to spend additional time refining your approach and can begin to build a reputation and later decide that you don't need the site anymore to book work.

The short answer is that, yes, you can book virtual assistant work on Upwork. It's one of the easiest ways to test the waters and begin looking for opportunities.

I even have a special method I teach my students about the best way to land your first job on Upwork to start making a killing over there if you so desire. It's a method that propelled me from $200 in earnings to $1200 the following month and $2400 the month after that.

The cool thing about a site like Upwork is that it works as much or as little as you want it to. The ball is entirely in your court. For more information about Upwork, you'll need to check out my course, The Guide to Killing it, on Upwork. It's the soup-to-nuts course on leveraging this popular website and specific strategies I used to bring in over $400,000 in revenue since I joined a few years ago.

# Do You Need a Website?

All new virtual assistants have some hesitancy over whether or not it makes sense to build a website. If you're inexperienced in building a website, this can seem like added frustration, expense, and time you'd have to dedicate. However, there are multiple reasons why it makes sense to put together a virtual assistant website. This is why I have an entire section devoted to website training and simple tools you can use in my course, Your Way to VA(Found at bit.ly/lauravacourse).

What follows are four of the most common reasons you should consider putting together a virtual assistant website. Your website, when functioning properly, can help to make you money at all times. Most people don't want to pay someone to create a website. While that's certainly okay, you do need one. You don't need to pay someone to do this, either. You can learn to do it yourself and can pitch your newly acquired skill to clients!

Most of my advice for freelancers is you don't need a website. However, when it comes to VAs, it does make sense to build something simple on Wix or Squarespace to have a web presence. You don't need to spend thousands of dollars. There are four primary reasons why it's worth your time and money to build a website.

## It Shows That You're Credible

Suppose you've ever been contacted by someone you couldn't identify anywhere else on the Internet. In that case, you can certainly relate to a potential client's concerns when they can't find your website either. You can come across as a fly-by-night provider, even when it's untrue. The one exception to this is if another virtual assistant or quality client has referred you.

However, it's still a good idea to have a VA website so that you can forge a personal connection with a client. Because you're working virtually, having a picture on your website and providing some basic information about you can help to show that you're a real person and will increase the chances a client will want to work with you.

## Allows You to Share Content and Some of Your Personality with Potential Clients

Not every client is going to be the right fit to work with you. However, you want to be able to showcase your personality and skills on your website. For example, if you have testimonials from past clients or examples of successful campaigns you've run for others, you may wish to include this on your website.

This can be highly valuable when it comes to converting clients. Sharing content can indicate to a client that you're intelligent and have writing and editing skills. This certainly doesn't do any harm when you've published it on your website. You don't have to have a blog as a new virtual assistant, but it's certainly something worth considering.

## Allows You to Be Found in Search Engine Results

If you do the proper SEO optimization for your website, this gives you a higher chance of popping up in search engine results organically. Most people hiring VAs will attempt to find a VA through multiple avenues. One may head over to Google and type in the skills to pull up various virtual assistant companies. It's a good idea to have your site SEO optimized so that you have used the proper keywords and can draw these clients in and get an intake call setup.

## Gives Clients an Idea of What They Can Expect Before Working with You

One of the most important things to do as a new virtual assistant is to establish your unique value proposition- and you should have already completed that earlier in the book. This is what sets you apart from everyone else pitching themselves as a virtual assistant. Your website is your opportunity to do that.

Your website can reflect your style, working ability, and general philosophy as a virtual assistant. This gives clients a heads up about what it'd be like to work with you. For example, a website that highlights your drive to meet deadlines, this can help to forge that important relationship built on trust you'll need with someone considering hiring their first person over the Internet.

As you can see, these are a handful of the reasons why your VA website can become a money-making machine for you if you work it properly.

# Ways to Market for Your First Client

I hear this a lot: "How am I supposed to compete with more established virtual assistants? I haven't even landed my first client."

It's possible to land your first client without any direct VA experience, but you have to sweeten the deal for your clients.

## How to Land Your Very First Client

### # 1: Promotions

Tip number one is to offer a promotional deal. This means you're giving some benefit to the client to sign up with you right now. Now, promotional deals can look like anything. It might be turning a project around rapidly, offering them a 30-minute free strategy session on the phone to talk about their business needs, or perhaps offering a certain percentage off for them to take action and hire you today.

When you're trying to stand out in a marketplace with a lot of other VAs who have experience while you don't, one of the best ways to combat that is to be really mindful of how you present yourself. And giving yourself a little bit of an edge with a promotional deal can help the client think about saying yes to you when they've never had the opportunity to work with you before. So, that's a great tip to reinvigorate your business. If you've felt frustrated and pitch yourself and not landing clients, this is a great way to get back on track.

### #2: Free Work in Exchange for a Testimonial

Some people aren't comfortable with this, and that's okay, but I've seen a lot of VAs do it. They'll offer a certain amount of their time for free in exchange for a testimonial. Testimonials are powerful and visible social proof on your website. If I hire you, and you are exceptional, chances are good I'll give you a testimonial you can use on your website. So, people checking you out can feel as though your work has been validated, and others have had a positive experience.

So, I've seen VAs give a ten-hour monthly package for free for one month in exchange for a testimonial. And then, hopefully, they rebook that client on ongoing contracts. But it doesn't always turn out that way. It's not always a guarantee but worth trying.

## #3: Rely on Past Experience

Another thing you can do is rely on your experience outside the virtual world. Often, if you know that you can't compete with other people because they have more experience, you aren't selling yourself enough. You're allowing yourself to get stuck in this mindset of comparing despair. Though you may not have hands-on experience as a virtual assistant, there is a good chance that you have experience as an administrative assistant or in an office scenario that can easily translate over to a VA world. Still, you don't know how to go about doing that yet.

And that's okay. So, keep that in the back of mind—you probably have some experience even in a volunteer capacity where you've organized people, have done data entry, Internet research, or customer service. You can translate those things on your resume so that the client can see the connection between what you've done offline and what you can do online.

These are my three favorite tips because you've got to find a way to get your foot in the door, and usually after that point of landing your first client, delivering a positive experience to them means that it's so much easier to book future clients. They'll give you great testimonial. Hopefully, they'll hire you long term and refer you to others. Plus, now you have that all other important social proof for when other people hire you too.

# #4: Be Specific about Your Services

When looking to book your first client as a virtual assistant, it's important to make sure you're marketing your services well and representing your brand/business clearly.

One thing that often puts clients off hiring a VA is when virtual assistants aren't specific enough about their services on their websites and business cards. Usually, the term virtual assistant is broadly defined. To make sure you're booking the right type of client for your business and help them find you, try confining the term virtual assistant into something more specific that clearly describes the services you provide. Here are some examples:

- A Business Manager

- A Social Media Assistant

- A Pinterest Wizard

- A Sales Strategist

- An Editor

- A Web Designer

- A Business Consultant

- A WordPress Expert

- A Copywriter

- A Facebook Ad Manager

- A Launch Strategist

- A Webinar Technician

Tweaking your job title to look something a little more like these will help you find your ideal client. However, some people still search for the specific term "virtual assistant," so make sure you respond to this term too.

Tip: Embed the keywords related to your specific title and the keywords "virtual assistant" in your body text as much as possible to search engine optimize your website.

Now that you've made your role a little more specific, you can do some easy things to help book your first client!

## #5: Client Forms

You can help yourself by getting to know your potential client before conversing with them using client application forms. You'll be surprised how many clients you'll turn away along your business journey. Some clients simply aren't the right fit given the services you provide, and no matter how tempting the money may be, it's important not to force yourself into taking on a client you might not be able to help. To make sure you attract more clients while also making sure they're the ideal ones, use client application forms to refine your potential client list and learn more information. Make sure you ask for the below information on your form:

- Full Name
- Business Name or Website(s)
- Email
- Phone
- Time Zone
- Referral Source (How did they hear about you)
- What do they need assistance with?
- How many hours will they need?
- What is their budget?

Making things easier on your clients to provide information paves the path for a more natural interview. Once they've already had a good experience working with you, they'll be excited to get to know you more on the call.

# Succeeding in Your Virtual Assistant Interview

At some point in your virtual assistant experience, you're probably going to be asked to do an interview. If you're using job boards like Upwork, this may happen, but if you're recruiting clients privately or bringing in traffic from your website, you're almost definitely going to be asked to do a virtual assistant interview. Now, don't let this unnerve you; don't get overwhelmed with this.

A few things to note before you head into an actual interview with a client. Be ready to talk about your experience. If you're a brand-new VA and don't have experience yet, that's okay too. Think about the experience you've had in previous jobs, volunteer opportunities, or in education that could translate to being a virtual assistant. You might be familiar with certain types of software or programs because of past experience, even if you've never technically been hired as a VA. So, be prepared to answer these questions honestly but maintain in control of the interview yourself.

The next thing to keep in mind is besides competency or your ability to do the tasks at hand, the next most important thing is to discuss how you can take things off the client's plate.

Remember those emotional cues that cause someone to think about hiring a virtual assistant in the first place. Listen for those during the verbal conversation. They might be saying I'm overwhelmed; I'm spending too much time at my desk and know I'm doing things I shouldn't do. Start taking notes during this conversation about things you may be able to take off the client's plate. The client can't mentally be in the position of thinking about hiring you and spending money on a virtual assistant if they don't see how they can help. So, this should be an ongoing conversation between the two of you about how you can contribute and make their life much easier.

As you talk with the client, take notes about what you can potentially do to help them, especially if they're bringing up tasks they didn't originally mention.

Here are some general tips for you when it comes to preparing for the interview:

- Use a professional scheduler like Calendly if the client doesn't have one (This helps you showcase your organizational skills too!)

- Have a professional atmosphere around you for the interview, like a quiet room and good lighting for video interviews

- Test all the tech you're using before you show up to the interview so that there are no problems on the day of the interview

- Be prepared with a 30-second elevator speech to discuss your background in case the client kicks off the call with "So, tell me a little bit about you."

- Try a practice interview with a spouse or friend. Once they've already had a good experience working with you, they'll be excited to get to know you more on the call.

## Tips for Marketing in "Facebook Groups"

"Facebook groups" are great places to research your ideal clients, but it can quickly become a race to the bottom when you're competing against dozens of other virtual assistants. If you do some research inside Facebook, you'll find plenty of different groups where you might find sources of leads. Remember that you're not the only virtual assistant using that particular method. When someone posts a need for a virtual assistant in these groups, they often receive dozens or even hundreds of replies. If you do spot a job offer in a "Facebook group," it's important to follow the directions for the person who posted it. If they know they only want you to apply through their Google form or by sending an email with certain instructions, don't deviate from that request.

You'll find yourself lost in their inbox or annoyed with your inability to follow instructions. It's hard to compete if you can't position yourself effectively. In these "Facebook groups," you'll also find that in many cases, one person comments and names or tags another virtual assistant they've worked with personally. This is the gold standard for effectively using "Facebook groups." Don't assume that the vast majority of your new or ongoing clients will come from "Facebook groups". You need to brand yourself, sending pictures regularly, and connecting with new people every single week. While it's certainly true that you might be able to land new clients from a "Facebook group" from time to time, it has become so competitive in most of these groups that it isn't a reliable source of ongoing leads.

Here are a few other tips to remember when leveraging Facebook groups:

- Don't private message somebody unless they've asked for you to do that.

- Speak directly to what the client has asked for. Don't only suggest they go look at your website. Respond with your experience/interest level in the tasks the original poster requested.

- Make sure you have a professional-looking profile picture

- Respond quickly when a lead is posted in a "Facebook group"; if you're the 100th commenter, there's a good chance the poster won't even get to your info.

# 8
# GETTING PAID

AT THIS POINT, you might wonder how to get clients. That chapter is next, but first, you need to have a decent idea of pricing. You don't want to end up on a call where the client is ready to hire someone and then lose your negotiation power because you have no idea what to charge. A firm grasp of your pricing will make all aspects of marketing from branding yourself on LinkedIn, or a website, to sales calls go more smoothly.

Don't let pricing or packages be a big stumbling block. In this chapter, you'll learn more about some of the basics behind pricing and how to create packages or hourly blocks for clients that sell.

To be successful with this, think like a client. What does a client want? What are the pitfalls with certain kinds of charging methods? How can you set up your business to protect you and appeal to the kinds of clients you're hoping to work with?

# Choosing Your Starting Hourly Rate

While there are many part-time jobs out there with a starting hourly rate of $10 or $12, I encourage you to think bigger. As a self-employed person, you're responsible for setting your rate by taking into account business expenses (like your Internet, your home office's portion of the utility bill, your website maintenance fees, PayPal fees, and many more.) You're also responsible for paying your taxes. In 2020, I'd recommend the absolute minimum hourly rate is $15 if you have limited experience.

You need to set your initial hourly rate higher to accommodate that you're now a business owner rather than an employee in someone else's business. Since the IRS considers you self-employed when you make any more than $600 per year, it's a good idea to start with the fact that you're a business owner from day one and charge accordingly.

A good minimum for your hourly rate is $15. From here, I'd consider pushing that rate up if you have special experience or software training that calls for you to do that. This isn't to say that you have to start at this hourly rate. There are plenty of entrepreneurs and business owners who are very comfortable paying $20 and $25 an hour for a new VA.

## Is Hourly Pricing the Right Fit?

The easiest thing to do for a new virtual assistant is to charge an hourly rate that's billed to the client after the work has been completed. Of course, this means you need to have a contract in place and trust that the client will indeed pay their bill when they receive it.

Here's what is challenging about open hourly invoicing: clients don't love it. In fact, some of them hate it because they've been a victim of "surprise billing" before. Here's what surprise billing means- the business owner or manager hires a VA or other freelancer to do a project. When they get it in their head that the rate is $15 or $20 an hour, the client often forgets to figure out how that might translate to a bill of $100 or more. If you and the client are not upfront in setting boundaries or caps on certain projects, you could have made big headway into a project before submitting a $500 bill, but to the client it feels like that $500 bill came out of nowhere.

No matter whether you're billing hourly one hour at a time or selling packages, have an upfront conversation with every client. Ask them if you should stop at a certain point if you spend more than X hours on a certain project. You can also give estimates to a client when you start a project so that they know upfront exactly what you're likely to spend your time and energy on. It doesn't have to be a perfect estimate, either, but it's great to give them a clear range.

Often relationships break down with clients because it's too awkward for the client to bring up that they weren't expecting such a big bill. It's on you as the VA to set realistic expectations and avoid that situation altogether.

## Reasons to Package Your Services as a Virtual Assistant

Once you've determined the appropriate virtual assistant rate for you, it's a good idea to package your work into several different options for your clients. Allowing them to purchase a package of hours has many various benefits and clarifies expectations upfront. What follows are four of the most common reasons to offer a package to your virtual assistant clients.

## It Makes Things Easier for Your Clients to Know What's Included

Most virtual assistants will offer a package of:

- 5 hours
- 10 hours

- 20 hours

- 40 hours

This allows a client to understand the various levels at which they can choose to work with you and shows that you don't accept smaller or bigger projects. This means that you can set up an hourly package that makes the most sense for you.

For example, if you're booked with other clients, you may not have the capability to take on a 40 hour a month client, but you can easily update these ordering buttons on your website to reflect that.

If you choose not to work with packages and complete a project for ten hours, but you still need a couple of hours to wrap the project up, you'd then have to email the client, wait for them to purchase additional time, and spend unnecessary time going back and forth with the client.

When a client has purchased a package of hours, you can update them once a week or once every couple of weeks about how those hours have been spent. This lets them know when they need to purchase more time.

Although you may still need to go back to the client to request more time on bigger projects, or if something is more in-depth than either of you originally anticipated, there is less of a chance doing this when you offer hourly packages.

## Your Clients Can Decide How Much or How Little of Your Time That They Need

This gives your clients the flexibility to start working with you in a smaller capacity and then be thrilled with your services. In turn, they choose to upgrade. For example, a client might purchase a five hour/month package and then decide the work you've done is so amazing, he or she wants to bring you on in a bigger capacity.

Giving your clients a taste test like this shows them how you work and the benefits of outsourcing particular aspects of their businesses. This works well with someone who's never had a virtual assistant before. Someone who's never had a virtual assistant in the past may not realize the benefits of working with someone in this capacity. If their time is freed up to do other things while you're taking care of administrative tasks and research, they might see the benefit of bringing you on in a more expensive package.

## You Can Bill Once or Twice a Month and Minimize Your Own Admin Time

One of the biggest reasons to offer hourly virtual assistant packages is you get paid upfront. This means that you're not completing a 40-hour project for a client and then waiting for him or her to come through with the payment.

You require your clients to purchase blocks of hours upfront, and when those hours expire, you can go back to your clients to ask for them to renew or for another package. This minimizes the amount of back and forth time you have to spend with invoices and clarifies expectations upfront about what you'll be working on.

When you offer specific hourly packages, your clients can ask how much you think you can complete in a certain block of hours. This allows you the opportunity to start off on the same page and minimize the potential for conflict.

Think about the packages you'd like to offer to clients today. If you're providing bigger packages, consider including a discount like 5% or 10% for those who purchase higher hours. This rewards them for their business and their investment in you.

Suppose you're focused on a particular type of niche, like being a Pinterest VA. In that case, you might roll all of your Pinterest services into one monthly retainer and include all your daily pinning and activities within it. However, if you're doing many different types of tasks, it makes sense to package your work hourly. You might include a ten, 20, 30, or 40-hour package and discount it, so there's an incentive for them to jump to the next level. You can start setting your most expensive hourly rate at the lowest possible number, allowing them to get ten hours of your time every single month, and adjusting it later as you move into the higher tiers.

When you're packaging your work, make sure it's crystal clear to the client exactly what is included in the package. If there are extras they'd need to pay for, such as your time on the phone to discuss the strategy on a project, make sure you reference what the hourly rate for that would be. It's also important to have the payment terms clear concerning a package. For example, somebody on a retainer might need to pay on that package by a certain date every month. Keeping your clients informed and giving them multiple package options to choose from helps them navigate through what they need a little easier.

To start with packages, keep it simple and come up with three options. These can be for blocks of hours, such as ten, 20, and 30. You can use blocks of hours that roll over into other months, or you can require that clients purchase a set block monthly.

# Important Tips to Keep in Mind with Packages

When you package your work like this, it's the same as if you're paying an attorney on retainer. You agree that they have $500 on hold with you for that month. All that work could come in the last week, or all of it could come in the first week. Or it can be spread out through the month. When they use up all of the prepaid hours, they'd need to roll into another package.

One of the reasons this works so well is because clients like to know what they're getting up front. Having it in a specific dollar amount package lets them know they can fit it into their marketing and employee budget for the month. It allows you to showcase your skills, and you want to accurately keep track of all the hours you work for a client in any one of these packages—you want to show them that value.

Project-based packages can work, too, if you're uncomfortable doing an hourly package. This will apply if a client contacts you to say, "I have XYZ project to send out 200 emails to various people. I don't know how long it's going to take, but I just want all of the project done."

In that case, you want to get as much information as possible about the project. You want to take a little bit of time to think about how long you realistically think it could take you to complete this entire project. Then, you want to give them a quote for a project base. Quoting as a project is hard for new VAs because you don't know how long certain things will take you yet, which is why quoting a range of hours with a set hourly rate is a good place to start with. Once you know more about how much of your time certain work takes, you can transition to project or retainer pricing.

A situation like this puts the client and the VA in a very awkward position because you don't want to have to start questioning someone's hours and the time they're spending on something. That is an inefficient use of a client's time. And yet, for some reason, the hourly work arrangement almost always seems to translate to this.

## Reasons to Get Paid Upfront

If you're establishing your career as a virtual assistant, one of the most common questions I receive is how to get paid. Certainly, your primary goal should be landing clients and giving them an amazing experience. Still, it's valuable to get paid upfront as a virtual assistant to avoid a lot of problems and frustration.

Nearly every new virtual assistant has some missteps, and everyone I've talked to has a horror story about doing work and never—yes, I said never—getting paid for the work. The best way to protect yourself from this is to use upfront payments from your client.

Now, if you do get paid upfront, I only recommend doing this at first for a small amount to give you and the client some freedom to end the contract if it's not a fit. If you pay a $1,000 deposit and learn it's not the right fit, you'll have an angry client demanding a refund. You can use a retainer once you've had the opportunity to work together, but I recommend spending a couple of hours on a project or doing a $100 job to ensure payment. Of course, you want to get this payment at the outset of the project. This is a great way to show your client good faith and payment for your work!

Here's what you need to consider in terms of establishing your payment guidelines:

Many virtual assistants ask their clients to purchase a package and pay for that bulk package upfront. This package might be a block of hours or one month's worth of work. So, a VA who works on retainer might charge $1000 for one month's worth of work up to a certain number of hours. Or they may charge a set amount for ten hours of work. It's then your job to keep track of your hours as you go. Here are a few reasons why upfront payments make sense.

## Upfront Payments Are a Sign of Good Faith from the Client

Never allow a potential client to take advantage of you. If you're going to do a tremendous amount of work—ten or 20 hours worth—you need a signal from the client that they intend to pay you. Unfortunately, some dubious and dishonest people are online, so it's a better protection tool to use upfront payments. It ensures that you do get paid even if the client disappears in the middle of the project. Maybe your pay won't reflect all owed but a majority of it.

## Getting Paid Upfront Puts a Responsibility on the Virtual Assistant

Certainly, the ball is in your court when you get paid upfront by a virtual assistant client, but if you don't show quality work, the client won't hire you again. It's up to you to show the client value to keep that retainer or hourly package open. Some VAs grow complacent and count on that money each month but slip in their work quality. Make sure you're always keeping track of your tasks and showing the client how you can save them time, help them earn more money, or allow them to do other things with their lives.

If your client is nervous about this initial engagement, offer a small paid trial period to determine if you're the right fit.

Now that you have a baseline for what to charge, let's dive into one of my favorite subjects, putting contracts in place to protect you.

Whether a job as a VA is new to you or not, you might not realize you need a virtual assistant contract to protect both you and your client. You'll have to fill out additional documentation for tax purposes or a nondisclosure or confidentiality agreement so that you don't share private details of their businesses.

# Benefits of Putting Together a Contract for VA Services

Even with all that paperwork, you'll still need a virtual assistant contract too. Contracts might seem like something only necessary for major corporations. Still, freelancers also need them for a broad range of reasons, and you may wish to consult with a business attorney to have one drafted for you.

You can also create a contract, but it could be invalid if it isn't compliant with state and federal laws. That's why it might be worth your time to put together a basic contract when you get started but set up a meeting with a business attorney to evaluate a more comprehensive contract. There are three primary reasons why virtual assistants need to consider putting together a contract.

## Gives You an Out If the Relationship Isn't Working

Many standard virtual assistant contracts require a notice to cancel the contract. This gives you time to close out any remaining projects and to locate an additional client to replace that stream of income, if necessary.

Your contract should clarify the reasons for which either one of you can terminate the relationship. Most standard contracts include verbiage that the contract can be canceled with a 15- or 30-day notice.

Having your clients pay in advance by using hourly packages is one way to ensure your income and make sure you're paid for the completed work listed in the contract.

## Contracts Ensure That Clients Know You're Serious

A contract is a formal agreement where both you and the client clarify expectations and your working relationship.

Although neither would ever want to visit small claims court to fight over this contract, it does help to add a layer of professionalism to your working relationship. For example, at some point, if the client isn't compliant with his or her end of the contract, you can reference the specific sections in the agreement and provide them the option to exercise the termination clause if they wish.

Far too many problems between virtual assistants and their clients have to do with a lack of clear expectations and communication. So, getting on the same page as your client from the outset can help avoid this problem completely.

## Addresses Payment Issues

One of the most important aspects of your virtual assistant contract regards the payment system. When will you receive payment? How will late payments be treated? And at what point will legal action be necessary?

Some clients might not realize that invoices need to be paid within seven days. Using terms inside your contract related to payment helps protect you and ensure clients know what's reasonable.

As mentioned above, so many problems with relationships between virtual assistants and their clients come back to communication problems. So, it's better to have this detailed information upfront. Make sure your client has read the contract, and you may wish to point out specific sections for clarity from day one. As you can see, any small business owner, even a solo virtual assistant, can benefit from using a virtual assistant contract.

# Common terms inside virtual assistant contracts

## Non-compete

A non-compete is an agreement between you and a client means you agree not to seek out your client's clients. This is most applicable in situations in which your role as a virtual assistant exposes you to the knowledge of your clients' customers and industry contacts. More often than not, a non-compete agreement is used outside of the digital world to ensure that a person doesn't come into a traditional job, learn everything there is to know about that industry and how to service clients, and then quit to poach all of the previous employers clients or contacts.

Nine times out of ten, a non-compete won't apply to your relationship with a client. The exception to this is when you're working for a virtual assistant agency. Working for a virtual assistant agency is one of the easiest ways to break into the marketplace because marketing is done for you on behalf of the agency. As a subcontractor in this agency, you're responsible for logging hours or completing projects at an agency rate. You can see why a company in this position might want to use a non-compete agreement to ensure you don't start your venture competing with them.

In general, you should consult with an experienced employment attorney if you see a non-compete clause in a virtual assistant contract. State laws apply, but judges tend to override non-compete agreements considered to be too restrictive. For example, a judge is unlikely to see any terms inside such an arrangement that prohibits you from working as a virtual assistant at all for two years after you complete your projects with the agency. At the same time, it might be reasonable for the company to ask you not to contact any of their clients for two years. After you jump ship to work on your own, a judge is likely to see it as too restrictive to ask that you don't work as a virtual assistant at all.

Read through the fine print to make sure you get an attorney's inside over whether or not a non-compete agreement truly represents what's fair and likely to be valid based on current laws.

## Payments & Contracts

One of the most important components that cause conflict between clients and virtual assistants is the payment terms. Your payment terms should include details about when payment is due, the methods through which the client can receive invoices and make payments, how late payments will be handled, and whether money will be owed to you if the project is suddenly canceled.

Even though this might seem like an extra expense as you launch your virtual assistant business, seek out resources that have templated contracts or hire a business attorney you can use in the future for each client. Your contract dictates terms of your working relationship, and it also becomes an important document to refer to if your client accidentally violates it. Imagine your client is five days late on their payment. If your client has signed a contract agreeing to pay a $25 late fee or 5% of the invoice amount, you can direct them to this line in the contract when reminding them to make a prompt payment before you assess the late fee.

Most of the payment terms included in a virtual assistant contract are designed to protect and encourage the client to comply with prompt and clear payment. You might request that your client purchase ten-hour blocks of your time. As a virtual assistant, you'll be responsible for keeping track of the time used on their project and letting them know when they're getting close to running out of your blocked time. If you're invoicing after the fact, it's your responsibility to set up clear payment terms with your client to pay for the work you've completed. You probably don't want to agree to a monthly invoice if you have to wait 30 days to get paid for all of the work you completed the month before.

# 9
# YOU'VE GOT A CLIENT: NOW WHAT?

THIS IS EXCITING! You've landed your first possible client, but now you have to follow up. Don't let your mindset talk you out of sending a proposal and putting together a client package. In this chapter, you'll learn more about what you need to do after a client has expressed interest in working with you.

On your sales call and immediately after, there's a chance to gather information from your client to help position yourself as the expert and make it an easy yes for your client to work with you.

If the client has decided to work with you, there's a few things you want to hammer out as soon as possible. These include

- The instructions and access you need to do the work

- How you'll be paid and when

- What constitutes completion of the tasks or project

- Where you should submit work

The excitement of landing a new client shouldn't gloss over the importance of doing these things. The more you can set the professional tone from the outset, the easier it becomes for the client to feel less nervous about what might, for them, feel like hiring a stranger on the Internet.

To the extent possible, make sure that the issues discussed in this chapter are covered in your contract with your client. The contract is your agreement about how the relationship will work. It's a powerful document to return to if you have a client who forgets the terms you originally discussed or deviates from the contract. The contract is covered first here, but all the other elements should be referenced within it.

# Get a Signed Contract

You should never perform work for a client without the support of a contract. The contract formally defines the relationship between the two parties and is your roadmap for all the terms of working together. Without a contract, you have no ground to stand on if there's been a misunderstanding or other issue.

You might be thinking that the core purpose of a contract is to give you legal ground to stand on when the other person doesn't hold up their end of the deal. But contracts are the words of agreement between you and the client and might come up during the working relationship and especially when it's ended.

If you don't have a written contract, it's anyone's game. Maybe you verbally agreed that your package hours didn't roll over from month to month, but if there's no contract, you could have an angry client claim they never knew, and it was never discussed. The bottom line is you need the contract to protect yourself.

Most clients don't read the contract with a fine-toothed comb, but it's there for both of you and clarifies any confusion when a client doesn't understand cancelation fees, notice required to end the contract, or how and when payment has to be sent to you.

Imagine a simple contract clause that says after payment is seven days overdue, you stop work, and all amounts owed up to that point must be paid in full with a 25% late fee before you'll do anything else for that person. If a client asks why their tasks haven't been completed after ignoring your invoice reminders, it's very simple to direct them to the contract's exact clause. Some clients might otherwise claim ignorance. Contracts make things crystal clear because they're in writing, dated, and both parties have to sign them before the work starts. There isn't confusion or surprises if the contract is signed.

I strongly recommend hiring a freelance lawyer to draw up a contract you can use more than once. You can hire one on Upwork.com Please also check out this link for Maryam Tsaturyan's resources where you can pay for contract templates you can use multiple times in your business with each client: https://bitl.y/34qb3eR

Get a physical signature or use something like HelloSign or Dubsado to get the contract signed, and keep it on file. If the contract needs to be renewed, set a calendar reminder, and get back to the client about updating the document for your continued partnership. If they decide not to work with you again, allow time to wrap up their pending projects.

Since I'm not an attorney (nor do I play one on TV), I can't give you legal advice. What follows are some recommendations, but these do not constitute legal advice. They're just great things to keep in mind when looking at a client-provided contract or to review one from your lawyer:

- What are the payment terms? When will you be paid, and by which method? Is all this information correct if the client provided the contract?

- How much lead time do you have to receive or provide if you decide not to work with this client any further? This is known as the cancel notice and can be anywhere from a few days to a month. It's awkward working for a client for a month after one of you has decided to end the relationship, so I suggest shorter timeframes.

- Confidentiality and non-compete issues: if you've received a contract from your client rather than the other way around, read the fine print on these sections. You might not be able to disclose that you're working with this client, or you might be signing something that says you can't work with any of their competitors for a certain period. There's usually room for negotiation if the non-compete terms seem unfair.

- How long does the contract last for? Once this current contract expires, what are the methods through which you can renew that contract?

- What methods, if any, will be the way you resolve disputes? Mediation? Arbitration? Court? It's unlikely you'll need to exercise any of these, but it's important to make sure the terms are reasonable, especially if you and the client live in different states.

You should never start working with someone if you haven't received a signed and dated contract for them.

# Getting the Right Instructions and Access

I can't stress the importance of instructions enough. All too often, relationships between VAs and clients fall apart due to communication problems.

Hop on the phone if you need to, get written instructions, type up a sheet of instructions and have them look it over. This is a good chance to make sure you're on the same page when you begin work together. It isn't a good idea to start work on a project, make all the decisions yourself, and then come back to the client.

The right instructions also include getting the passwords you need so you can access whatever part of their website, social media, email list, or another tool that's required for you to do the job. If this is the client's first time working with a VA, inform them of tools like LastPass and Dashlane. These tools allow the client to share a secure login to a team member where you don't even need to see the client's password. This is a secure and straightforward way to get access quickly, so let them know which email address you want to be used for this purpose.

# How You'll Be Paid and When: Invoicing as a VA

There are so many details to take care of when you're starting a new career as a virtual assistant and launching out on your own. It can seem tempting to gloss over some of the less important aspects from your perspective. While there are certain things you need to focus on more closely than others, thinking about how you can put together and send invoices to your clients isn't one of them. Coming up with a streamlined program well in advance of booking your first client will make it that much easier.

Ultimately, the goal is that you'll be fully booked with work and will need to have a streamlined invoicing system in place. Otherwise, you run the risk of becoming disorganized and forgetting to invoice clients. This is much more likely to happen when you're booked with a great deal of business and spend a lot of your time working on client projects. You should always track your time, of course, but you should also think carefully about invoicing and how you can do it most effectively.

## Invoicing as Part of Administrative Time

You'll need to set aside time each week to invoice your clients, and you'll also need to have clear invoicing terms set up well in advance. I recommend setting aside one-half day each week to deal with your invoices. This is a great time to touch base with clients who have overdue invoices, put together invoices into an automated system if you have one, and send out any invoices. I usually allot the mornings on Friday to this task to cross it off my list for the week.

## What Kind of Invoicing Software Should I Use?

Many people find it free and easy to use PayPal's built-in invoicing software. You can easily link your PayPal account to any number of bookkeeping programs, and it's always easy to go in and see what's been paid. Under a business account on PayPal, you'll also see a note in the lower-left corner when you log in that says how many unpaid invoices are currently pending.

This is a great way to check and send simple reminders. Of course, you can also use various invoicing applications, but you may need to pay for some of these services. Frankly, I've found that keeping it all in one place in PayPal makes my life a whole lot easier because I don't have to click and open multiple websites. My clients can easily link their checking accounts or their credit card information to invoicing.

## What Does Your Time Tracking Management Have to Do with Invoices?

If you aren't working on package-based programs where you're going to be billing a client regularly for a retainer amount, you must keep track of your time. I strongly recommend that you include plenty of information about what was done during that specific period in your invoices to clients. For example, you might have notes like "Tuesday, 2-4pm, two total hours scheduling social media posts." Keeping this for your records is valuable enough, but it becomes even more important when you're translating this information over to an invoice. Bear in mind that many clients are busy, and even when they're giving you plenty of tasks, they may not remember everything you've been working on. Putting these details into an invoice makes things a lot easier for your clients so that they can quickly review and pay the invoice.

## What Are Invoicing Terms and Why Should I Care?

Across the freelance industry, you'll see a broad range of invoicing types. Some people request invoices be paid within three days. Others request they're paid within seven days. Some individuals invoice on the first of every month and request payment by the fifth of that month. I strongly recommend having a five to seven-day window for your clients to pay their invoices.

This gives them plenty of time to review the work and come back with any questions. Try to always send your invoices to your clients on the same day of the week. For example, you might do this on Monday after you've completed the previous week's work, or you might do it on Friday nights to indicate all of the completed work. When your client starts to get invoices on different days, and it's not entirely clear what it's for, there's more likely to be an oversight and confusion that could delay the payment.

As a freelancer, you need to have a way to bill your clients. You not only want to be paid, but you want to be able to track your payments via invoicing systems. The following are some free or cheap invoicing systems that work great and are easy to use:

## PayPal

Very popular. Most people use PayPal and have access to it, making it easier, and one of the first choices for many. It's nice to have everything all in one place if you need to go back and look at anything. PayPal has a great search function that you can search for a specific amount of time or the name of a specific invoice or invoices. PayPal offers free invoices; you don't have to pay a fee to send the invoice. Like any other payment you receive on PayPal, there is a charged fee once you receive it.

## Wave

Wave is a great resource for freelancers that is a free option to send out invoices. You can create invoices very easily and customize the way they look. If you'd like to receive payments on Wave, there is a fee for accepting credit cards. That fee is 2.9% + 30¢ per transaction. The good thing is that you can accept payments directly from anyone who owns a credit card.

## FreshBooks

FreshBooks is easy to use, and it narrows down the time you spend creating invoices. One great thing about FreshBooks is you can see if your client has opened your invoice. Sometimes, clients say they don't receive the invoice. With FreshBooks, you know for sure. FreshBooks offers a recurring billing option so that you don't have to send out the same invoice every month. When it's time, the client automatically receives it, and you don't have to do anything! **FreshBooks** offers a free trial for you to try out their system. Then, you can choose the plan that works for the number of clients you have.

How you package and position your services can greatly impact the profitability of your freelance business. It's incredibly important for freelancers to speak about their pricing naturally and confidently. And while custom proposals can be a great option, they don't work as well in an impromptu conversation with a potential client at a networking event!

# How to Deal with Late Payments

Late payments can be a big problem for a VA. Running a business and getting paid means you can't afford to have a lot of clients who can't keep up with their payment terms. Of course, you want to have a great contract in place since this protects you. While some clients might actively attempt to evade payment, it's far better to leave room for the possibility that there was an honest mistake or oversight like an expired or stolen credit card.

If someone's payment is late, start with gentle reminders. Maybe an assistant deleted the email, or it went into spam. Always assume the best in this situation before putting on the pressure. But it's a good idea to pause on all work until the pay situation is corrected. This is especially true if it's been more than a few days since you sent your invoice reminder. If you can, pushing to see if they can give you a date to fix the situation. Note that and circle back if it hasn't been fixed yet.

Having a term for what happens when a payment is late gives you a place to start from; if you assess a late fee, reference that in the contract kindly by telling the client when it's about two days out from when that late fee will apply. Make sure the client understands the payment terms.

Even though I'm advocating for you to give your clients a chance to fix things within reason, know when to call it quits. If someone has paid their invoice late three times or you've had to chase them down, that isn't worth it. So, know when to call it quits and activate that termination clause in the contract. A client who causes you more trouble than he or she is worth is someone you need to let go because that influences your ability to pay your bills and keep your business afloat. Mistakes certainly happen, but if it's repeated mistakes, there's certainly something going on, and it's not fair to you to be involved in the middle of that.

# Other Issues to Discuss with Your Client First

You don't want to bombard someone with too much information, but it helps to get a few clarification concerns out of the way. Communication is vital during the early stages of this working relationship. What might otherwise be a minor understanding can blow up into the end of the relationship before you've had a chance to build trust with this new client.

## What Constitutes Completion?

Will you need to send a weekly report every Friday explaining what you did that week? Will your work be measured by a number, such as the number of social media posts scheduled or the number of rows entered into a spreadsheet? Clarify this upfront. You most likely don't need to track every single minute you spend on the client's project with a line-item explanation. This is annoying and overwhelming for most clients. But it's a good idea to dig into the details and ask the client how much information or reporting they'll need. A weekly report works well for most clients, so that's a good starting point if you don't already have something in mind.

## How Should You Submit Work?

Some clients might ask you to track your time. As a general rule, this is a good idea when you start your VA business so that you can hold yourself accountable and learn about how long it takes you to do certain tasks. I dislike using time tracking software that captures pictures of my screen as I'm working. Examples include the Upwork Time Tracker and Time Doctor. While I can see the benefit of these, I'm not open to giving my client license to capture whatever I'm doing on my screen (or the many other tabs I might have open at the same time that aren't any of their business.)

If your client is adamant that you need to track your time, here's what I recommend: offer to use a time tracking software for a few weeks to show you're getting work done. Then, switch to a model where you bill them for the time you worked. If you can't build a trusting relationship in a few weeks, this is a red flag.

You can always use time tracking software to see where you're spending your time and to hit start/stop for various clients. I like Toggl because it's free, and you can set up different labels for all your different clients or projects.

If you can, help your client get out of their email inbox. Delivering projects over email is very ineffective for both of you when your client is already busy. And chances are good your client is busy enough to recognize they need to hire a VA, so help them use free tools like Google Suite (documents and spreadsheets with comments) or Trello so they can see the status of a project without problems.

When you first begin working together, ask the client how and when they should be notified that you're either done with a project or stuck on one. I use a Trello board for my VAs that has a list called "help—needs Laura's review" and "complete." This tells my VAs exactly where to put their work and how to tag me.

If your client doesn't already have a process in place, suggest one. Remember, a big reason why clients hire VAs is to help them stay organized.

One of the best things my executive assistant, Melissa, did when she first started working with me was to go through every open project, spreadsheet, and process I had. It helped her get a sense of where projects were and spot the gaps and make recommendations for improved processes. This took us two weeks, but we were then able to start implementing more effective plans for making sure projects get done, and we didn't miss deadlines. For me, as a client, it's well worth it to have a virtual assistant who steps up to the plate to make recommendations about how to streamline things. Keep these organizational skills in your back pocket since working for a client isn't only about completing the tasks, they give you—saving them time, energy, and frustration goes a long way towards building a long-term relationship with someone!

## Communication with Clients

As a client, I hate it when people send me unnecessary emails. I'm constantly struggling to get my unread messages under 100, so I don't need random emails unrelated to my current priorities. But as a VA, you also need a place to reach out if there's something urgent, like a big customer demanding a refund, your VA suddenly locked out of an account, or someone hacked your website.

It's a good idea to discuss this upfront to know which forms of communication to use for various issues. Your project management board might be the main place to store documents and post status updates, but if something more urgent comes up, do you reach out over the phone? Slack? Voxer? Email? It's always good to know this before a concern like this emerges so that you have a plan in place.

Now that you've laid the groundwork with your client for an effective relationship, it's time to work!

One of the hardest things to do as a new virtual assistant or freelancer is getting your first client. It's often the hardest to do this because you feel a lack of confidence about what you're doing and aren't sure of the marketing channels that will bring you the most business and the most qualified business to build your company. So, that lack of confidence translates to how you market and the type of clients you land.

But the first couple of clients that you work with are important for your credibility because they can lead to multiple referrals or even testimonials that land future work. They also build your confidence for future marketing. Even if you're doing one-off projects or a situation where the client asks you to work on a particular project from beginning to end and then has you wrap up with them, that doesn't mean that all of the money-making potential with that client is complete. Clients can be a really powerful source of referrals and testimonials.

Now, clients who have a positive experience working with you are much more willing to refer you to someone else. When someone posts in a "Facebook group" that they're looking for a virtual assistant to help with a particular task, five or ten people who tag someone else in the comments to that Facebook post. That's a direct referral and a recommendation from someone else. That kind of social proof goes a long way when you're a new virtual assistant or freelancer of any type because it's hard to give a stranger over the Internet your money. Bringing on a new team member, especially if it's the client's first hire as a virtual assistant, is a nerve-wracking experience. They want to know that they're going to get high quality and what they're paying for. But having someone else jump in and say, 'Hey, I had a positive experience working with this virtual assistant. I recommend them as a go-to source of information and high-quality work." That speaks volumes to your potential clients.

In the same way, positive comments from your clients on job platforms such as Upwork help other people see that clients have had a positive experience working with you and can crack open the door for future work with those clients and other clients. You should never view a wrapped-up job as one-and-done because the potential for referrals and testimonials is always there. Sometimes, you have to ask. In many cases, clients don't know how important it is to a virtual assistant or freelancer to build on testimonials and referrals. But if they've been thrilled with the experience of working with you, they're much more likely to give you those testimonials and referrals. Be prepared to ask.

When you finish up a job with a client or while you're in an ongoing contract of retainer work with a client, let them know how much feedback and testimonials help you land other clients and how important it is you're doing a good job for them. Usually, they'll be more than happy to provide you with a couple of sentences about what it's been like to work with you. You can use this on your testimonials page or a one-sheet. You can add this to your LinkedIn profile and use it in different ways. It continues to pay off for you when other people have good things to say about your work and overall experience. You can use this to build your referral business one client at a time.

One of the things I like is to have a referral program in place. For every one of my coaching or freelance clients who refer another person to me, I pay out $200 to the referral source when the new clients buy any package at $1,000 or more. Promoting this to my clients gives them an easy reason to develop a solid client recommendation for me. Since your ideal clients are likely to refer you to other people like them, you can build your clients' base over referrals while also being active with other marketing efforts.

So, now you know how to market and set yourself up for success with your new client from the very first day. What's next? In the following chapter, you'll discover more about how to avoid the most common mistakes.

# 10
# NEXT STEPS: TOOLS, TRICKS, & SOFTWARE TO LEARN

ONE OF THE core components of this chapter is reviewing all the most popular software most virtual assistants should consider learning; however, this is only one part of this idea of getting started with your next steps. Starting and growing your virtual assistant business requires you to keep on top of trends and always learn new things. Consider the fast pace of technology and how it calls on all of us to pick up new skills and software—new jobs and areas of specialization for virtual assistants are created all the time.

# How to Create a Simple Virtual Assistant Website

The virtual assistant industry is expected to grow by at least 4% from 2018 to 2022. It's one of the thriving online industries even in the face of global pandemics like the COVID-19 outbreak. Starting out as a virtual assistant means you have to get everything right while running a tight budget. A website is one of the few resources that offer a higher ROI while costing little. Here is a comprehensive guide on how to get one.

## Why Do You Need a Virtual Assistant Website?

For a business primarily done from home, a website is a must-have because of the following reasons:

### 1. Presence and Brand Building

It's the only way to build a substantial online presence before you branch out to social media channels. These other options will echo what you have on the website. By having your domain name, logo, and colors, you can create a brand and build on it to get more clients and differentiate yourself.

### 2. Marketing Strategy

Your marketing strategy is to drive leads to your website from where they can order your services. Without a website as an anchor, your online marketing strategy will be handicapped and less effective.

### 3. Increase Market Reach

A website exposes you to the millions of people and online companies that need your services. You can build your local and international reach from the same platform at no extra cost.

### 4. Easy Access

Your clients and potential clients can easily find you and your services whenever they search online. Even when you're away, the site still works for you, informing them of your offering, contacts, and rates.

### 5. Professionalism

Having a website is presently one of the basic requirements of any serious business. Lacking one puts off many clients, especially those seeking a virtual assistant. You can't be trusted with a clients' needs if you display such disregard to your own.

### 6. Demonstrate Your Work

Finally, a website allows you a platform to demonstrate your skills and what you'll offer potential clients. Clients get a preview of what you offer and your unique selling point.

## Elements of a Virtual Assistant Website

An Effective VA Website Should Have the Following Elements:

### 1. Excellent Navigation

On-page navigation and navigation across different pages has to be seamless and orderly. Quick page loading is also a factor, and there should be an accurate and comprehensive sitemap and page menu.

## 2. Services Offered Page

One of the sections you need is a services-offered page, which makes it easier for potential clients to determine if you'll serve their needs. It also offers you a chance to provide a description and accompanying rates for the service, helping with search engine optimization. If you've not heard of SEO before, it's a fancy way of discussing how Google and other search engines catalog your layout, keywords, and content. Listing out your services in bullet points helps make it visually pleasing for people who land on the site.

## 3. Contact Information

Contact information should be displayed on its own page, ideally accompanied by a form that makes it easy for clients to reach you. Provide your email address, phone number, and social media pages to give the prospective clients options to reach you.

## 4. About Us Page

This page is the biggest chance you have to sell yourself while linking your strengths to the needs of the clientele you want to attract. It should cover your story, unique selling points, skills, and everything else that'll make you stand out from the competition.

## 5. Testimonials/Portfolio Page

You're going to need proof of the quality of work you can offer. This evidence is either through a portfolio page or a testimonial page with reviews from former clients. You can have both and even include a couple of testimonials on the home page for a stronger first impression.

## 6. Quality Content

The content you have across the site should be top-notch to serve the purposes of addressing your client's needs, selling your services, and also to rank higher on search engine pages.

## 7. Calls to Action (CTA)

You want your site visitors to convert into clients, and you can only do this by directing them further down the conversion funnel. Have CTAs placed strategically across the site with a sense of urgency to get the leads to perform the desired action like hire you, sign up for a newsletter, make an inquiry, or call for a quote.

## 8. Blog

Your website needs a blog where you'll provide industry-relevant content to help you establish yourself as an expert in your field. It can also be used to get quality links to and from other sites in your SEO efforts.

## 9. Responsive Design

You need to have a responsive design because your prospective clients will access you from different devices. A responsive design allows all your information to be neatly presented even on smaller screens, and Google rewards mobile responsive sites with a higher ranking.

## 10. Newsletter for Signup

Finally, you need a newsletter that clients and prospective ones can sign up for. It allows you to create a mailing list you can use for your marketing purposes.

# How to Create a Virtual Assistant Website on a Budget

The challenge for anyone starting a business is budget, and it isn't good sense to splash money when you aren't receiving regular business. However, you can still get a competent and professional business site by following the steps below.

## 1. Hosting Package

First, find an affordable package that offers several benefits like a free domain name. Start with a basic package, and you can upgrade later when business demands it.

## 2. Website Builder

Choose the website builder you'll use on your site. The main ones currently are WordPress, WIX, Squarespace, and Weebly. WordPress is widely used thanks to the options it offers, but WIX and Squarespace offer smoother learning curves and ready themes that need minimal tweaking, which is excellent when you have no skills and no budget to hire someone.

Squarespace offers nice templates you can start with to build a site that looks like it was more expensive than it was. Its primary competitor would be WordPress, which must be installed on a domain and backed up by hosting. The cool thing about Squarespace is that your design plan paid monthly or annually includes the hosting, and you can even buy the domain simultaneously. That's a big reason why it's so popular.

## 3. Finding a Developer

If you need a developer, find freelancers like you in the job boards and marketplaces like Fiverr and Upwork, and choose one with good ratings who meets your budget. This is a more expensive route to go, but it might also mean less frustration for you if web development is not a skill set you already have.

## 4. Free Plugins /Free Fonts

You'll need plugins and proper themes to make the site professional. At the start, go for the free ones, and pick those with positive reviews. Settle on those which best match the image you want to portray.

## 5. Create Your Content

Finally, you'll have to create your content to be used on the site. You may have to do more research and brush up your writing skills, but this will help you save considerably on buying content or hiring someone.

Now that you know what it takes to get a bootstrapped website up and running, let's talk more about some of the things you might want to teach yourself in terms of software. These will help you get out ahead of the curve when talking with clients in showing you have the knowledge and a desire to learn.

For the section below, there are a lot of links to courses. As a result of that, you can find a PDF version of this section of the book with clickable links at www.virtualassistantbook.com

# Top Software Programs All New Virtual Assistants Need to Learn

## Canva

**What it is:** Canva is a free drag and drop graphic design tool. Easily create logos, social media posts, PDFs, flyers, proposals, and more in minutes. Completely customizable designs. Many clients you work for will have their own account or templates you can use to create their designs. There is also a paid version, which allows you to upload custom fonts and have access to more images for $12.99/month.

**Top free training:** Canva itself has *amazing training*! They have a design school with endless amounts of videos and training updated constantly.

**Affordable paid training:** *Skillshare* has a huge collection of Canva trainings that let you get specific about the things you want to create. Skillshare currently costs $15/month, and you can usually get your first month (or two) free.

## Adobe Spark

**What it is:** Adobe Spark is a free drag and drop social media post editor. Easily create Pinterest pins, social media posts, social media videos, and much more in minutes! It's easily customizable with brand colors and fonts and has a paid version with more features included in the *Adobe Creative Cloud.* Adobe Spark is the perfect way for beginners to jump into the world of social media post creation and video creation.

**Top free training:** *Digital Creations YouTube Video*

**Affordable paid training:** *Udemy - The Complete Adobe Spark Course, $11.99*

Looking for FREE stock photos for your design? Check out these sites:

Pixabay Pexels Unsplash

Also be sure to check out Creative Market on Mondays for free fonts, templates, and more!

Email Newsletters/Management

## Convertkit

**What it is:** Convertkit is an email service provider that provides powerful email automations and processes. It has integrations with top programs and software such as Shopify, Teachable, Leadpages, ClickFunnels, and SamCart. It has a visual editor, which it makes it easier to use than more complicated programs like Keap. The cost to get started is $29 per month, and you can usually get a month free if you can find a code.

**Top free training:** Redefining Mom has a great series of free Convertkit trainings. Find them *here*.

**Top paid training:** *Convertkit Club.* The cost is $20/month, and you can cancel at any time and includes "Facebook group," video training, Zoom Call, etc.

## Mailchimp

**What it is:** MailChimp is a very popular email marketing system. Part of the reason that it's so popular is that it's one of the few email systems that offer a completely free plan and other very affordable plans. For beginner VAs, this is great because you can sign yourself up for a free account and jump right in to learn a few things. MailChimp integrates with platforms such as Facebook, Canva, Zapier, and Shopify.

**Top free training**: Naturalvita offers a free, complete YouTube training *here*.

**Top paid training:** MailChimp themselves offers multiple classes on *Skillshare* on the different ways to utilize their program. Skillshare is $15/month for unlimited access to classes.

## Active Campaign

**What it is:** ActiveCampaign is an email marketing system that features automation and also CRM. Some of their pricing packages also include text messaging systems to keep track of your customers. Put all together, ActiveCampaign's processes provide a seamless process for the customer during every aspect of the customer journey. Pricing varies widely from $9/month up to $229/month!

**Top free training**: ActiveCampaign themselves offers an entire library of video training for free on their *website*.

**Top paid training:** *The Active Marketer* offers lifetime access to their complete paid training, which covers every aspect of ActiveCampaign – one- time fee of $37.

# Online Courses

## Teachable

**What it is:** Teachable is a platform for housing and creating your online courses. It's a great platform for beginner entrepreneurs because they have a free option. Now, keep in mind that the free account does take a percentage of your course fee with the free plan. If you upgrade to a larger plan, no fee is taken. Teachable allows you to have videos, worksheets, checkout pages, dripped content, and other features to make course creation easy.

**Top free training:** *YouTube Video: How to Create a Course in Teachable (full walkthrough)*

**Top paid training:** *Skillshare* has this great class. You can pay $15 a month for unlimited access.

## Thinkific

**What it is:** Thinkific is another online course platform. It is a little more in-depth than Teachable and doesn't offer a free version. Thinkific is completely customizable and has drag and drop features, making it ideal for course creators with little experience. It is integrative with Leadpages, MailChimp, Google Analytics, and many more. Pricing starts at $49/month, and they do have a free trial.

**Top free training**: The Social Launch has a step by step course creation video on *YouTube*

**Top paid training:** Udemy has a course called *Build Your Own Course Platform* on Thinkific for $11.99

## Clickfunnels

**What it is:** ClickFunnels is a sales funnel builder that helps entrepreneurs market their products to the customers through a "funnel" system. After that, ClickFunnels leads the customer through the entire process of selling and delivering products. This system works for both physical and digital goods. ClickFunnels ranges in price from $97 – $297/month.

**Top free training**: *Shawn Bayley* has an entire collection of free YouTube videos on how to use every aspect of ClickFunnels. **Top paid training:** There are all kinds of ClickFunnels trainings out there that cost a fortune. The most affordable are on Skillshare or Udemy. Udemy has a very high rated course called *The Ultimate ClickFunnels Training Course + Free Funnels* for $11.99

# Website Management

## Squarespace

**What it is:** Squarespace is a website host that features easy drag and drop options and customizable themes to make your website in half the time! You can buy your domain, choose your theme, customize your template, and be up and running in no time. There are options to add blogs, stores, and membership sites as well.

**Top free training:** Megan Minns has an entire *Teachable course* on how to use Squarespace with video walk-throughs - for free!

**Top paid training:** Honestly, there are so many free trainings, it's probably not worth it to pay for one! But if you do, there is a great Squarespace tutorial on *Skillshare.*

## Google Analytics

**What it is:** Google analytics is an analysis tool for your website. It can show you clicks, traffic, Pinterest traffic, and all kinds of data about what types of people are visiting your website. This can be very useful for entrepreneurs so that they can see where their traffic is coming from and take full advantage of it. They can also see where they need to improve. It is free when you own your own domain.

**Top free training:** Google itself has a *great training* on how to use their tool.

**Top paid training:** This is another program that has so many free trainings. It may not be worth it to pay for it. However, on *Udemy*, you can take a course to get certified, which could look great in your portfolio! Cost is $11.99.

## WordPress

**What it is**: WordPress is an open source website creation tool that is one of the most popular in the world. There are thousands of free and paid themes to make every website completely unique. It can be challenging to learn, but there are so many options to make it easier so that every VA can learn WordPress. WordPress has the option of adding additional drag and drop editors such as Beaver Builder and Elementor to make it an even easier process. WordPress itself is free, but you need to buy a domain and a host or use a WordPress hosted site. (i.e yourname.wordpress.com)

**Top free training**: WP Beginner has a *free course* (Learn WordPress for Free in a Week or Less)

**Top paid training:** LinkedIn Learning has several courses in their paid monthly plan, including a range of *WordPress Training and Tutorials.* Cost is $29.99/month. Skillshare and Udemy also have quite a few step by step tutorials.

# Project management

## Trello

**What it is:** Trello is a project management tool for teams and can also be used for individuals. It is set up in a board-style. You can make checklists and organize information into categories, assign members to a project, add documents, links, photos, and color-code tasks for easy management. Trello is free to use and has a gold plan that allows for certain things like uploading files greater than 10mb. It starts at $5/month or $45 per year.

**Top free training**: Paul Nicholson offers a 30-minute *free training* and walkthrough of Trello on YouTube **Top paid training:** Trello is another one of those platforms that you may not want to pay for free training, since there are large quantities of free training. Trello does offer a series of trainings on *Skillshare* that go into great depth on different uses.

## Asana

**What it is:** Asana is also a project and team management tool. You can create projects, assign tasks, assign due dates, and add all attachments needed to your team's space. Projects can be color-coded, and Asana tasks can be added from Gmail and Slack (a team messaging service). You can also set up notifications in the app or through email when tasks are assigned or due. Asana is also free to use but has a paid plan for large teams.

**Top free training**: Asana itself has a great step by step free *Academy* detailing the basics and all of the integrations that can be used with the software.

**Top paid training:** Udemy offers a *Fundamentals of Asana* for $11.99

## Basecamp

**What it is:** Basecamp is a project management tool that is similar to both Trello and Asana, but much more in-depth. Basecamp features live chat, scheduling, themes, and also a portal for clients to login. The thing that sets Basecamp apart from the rest is its price. It starts at $99/month, so it's a tool geared more towards running an entire team and clients.

**Top free training:** Basecamp itself has their own thorough *training*, including live classes that you can join in on.

**Top paid training:** LinkedIn Learning also offers a comprehensive *Basecamp tutorial,* included in the monthly fee of $29/month.

# Social Media Management

## Hootsuite

**What it is:** Hootsuite is a comprehensive social media management platform. You can use the platform to schedule all social media platforms including LinkedIn, Twitter, Facebook, Instagram, Pinterest, and YouTube. It includes analytics of your social media platforms and has integrations with Slack, Zapier, Trello, and more. Hootsuite has plans ranging from Free to $599+ /month.

**Top free training:** Hootsuite has their own free training *Academy* for using their platform.

**Top paid training:** Udemy has the highest-rated paid trainings, with *Social Media Optimization and Automation* with Hootsuite being the highest. Cost is $11.99

## Tailwind

**What it is**: Tailwind is a scheduling tool for social media that's mainly for Pinterest and Instagram. It offers a large array of Pinterest tools, including analytics, time optimization for pins, the ability to join tribes, and scheduling on SmartLoop. Tailwind is well known in the Pinterest scheduling world to be one of the best tools for getting the most out of your Pinterest account and driving traffic to your website or blog.

**Top free training:** Louise Myers has an in depth *blog post* detailing step by step how to use Tailwind.

**Top paid training:** With Tailwind having their own tutorials, and all of the free ones on YouTube, there isn't really a reasonably priced tutorial to recommend.

## Buffer

**What it is:** Buffer is also a social media scheduler and has been around for years. Its free plan will allow you to schedule three social media platforms, while the paid platforms offer up to unlimited platforms. Buffer also analytics and has a mobile app. It's very user friendly and has a simple interface.

**Top free training:** Udemy actually has a free course outlining how to use automations for social media.

**Top paid training:** Buffer is another one of those platforms that has unlimited free tutorials; it's actually difficult to find a paid one! Yay for free training.

# Other Software

## Zapier

**What it is:** Zapier is an integration tool. Even if apps don't have a direct integration, Zapier can create "zaps" to connect them and automate workflows. For example, if you get an email, you can trigger zaps in apps like Dropbox and Slack to save your information and alert you that you got the information. Zapier is free to start using and includes 5 zaps. As you add zaps, the price increases.

**Free Training**: Zapier has a *University* on YouTube, walking you through all that you need to know about the platform.

## Calendly

**What it is:** Calendly is a scheduling tool. It's immensely useful for scheduling things like Discovery calls and also managing your calendar. A lot of clients will have you manage their calendars for them, and this a frequently used tool by entrepreneurs. It can be embedded on websites, or you can put the link to your calendar in our email signature or on a Facebook page, so people can easily schedule time with you. It's very easy to use and integrates with quite a few other programs, such as Zoom, Salesforce, and Stripe.

**Free Training:** The Firehill Group has an easy step by step *tutorial* on how to use Calendly. It's meant for real estate agents, but their message is universal.

## Dubsado

**What it is:** Dubsado is a CRM (Customer Relationship Manager) that allows you to create workflows, capture leads, and create amazing customer experiences. You can also create branded invoices, proposals, and contracts. Dubsado is free for your first three clients, and then it costs $34/month

**Free Training:** YouTube has great walkthroughs on how to get started with Dubsado. Nesha Woolery has a great one to start with *here.*

## Getting More Help with Your VA Business

Did you know that as a reader of this book, you'll get exclusive access to a coaching session with me? We'll use this session to discuss your specific questions and create a 30-day action plan for you. These one-hour sessions are often all that a reader needs to jumpstart and boost your confidence that you're ready and capable to do this!

Here's how the session works:

- You'll sign up at www.virtualassistantbook.com

- You'll submit a copy of your current resume and up to five questions you have after reading this book. If you have website copy or LinkedIn profiles you need me to review before the session, please share that too.

- You'll show up to Zoom for our recorded coaching session. I'll have feedback for you based on the info you submitted, but we'll also talk through any other questions or concerns you have.

# 11

# COMMON VA
# PITFALLS

THE MORE YOU can set yourself up to avoid common pitfalls and challenges in your virtual assistant business, the more you'll be able to scale quickly and continue serving clients with as little downtime as possible.

## Four Things You Should Never Do as a VA

I've worked directly with a number of virtual assistants I've hired. Also, I've managed quite a few virtual assistants to carry out digital projects online, and unfortunately, some virtual assistants don't bring the highest level of professionalism to a job. There are several things I've noticed both in my experience and when consulting with other entrepreneurs about VA contributions. VA may be well-meaning, but it doesn't always lead the client to continue to trust you, and it can erode your relationship and end up terminating the contract. So, here are four things that I think you should never do if you are a new virtual assistant.

## Don't Avoid Blame When It's Your Fault

Everybody makes mistakes, including me. As a virtual assistant, you're going to make mistakes. There are going to be things that you could've handled better, or the client could've handled better, or people you wish you'd never worked with, but I don't like working with virtual assistants who never accept blame. These are the people who always have an excuse for why *it's not their fault*. Sometimes, they blame it on the client or use an excuse like "I was tired." Whatever it is, they never actually accept the blame for what they did wrong.

You know when you have a business and are helping somebody run their business as a VA, you have a responsibility to let them know what fell apart and how you're going to fix it in the future. Simply saying, "I'm sorry. I got tired and didn't get to it" doesn't cut it. That's not accepting blame.

There is a big difference between someone making the above statement and saying, "Hey, I'm really tired right now. It's my fault that I overbooked myself. I won't make that mistake again in the future. Next week, I've lightened my load to make sure that I get everything done on schedule." If the blame is yours, own it.

## Overbook Yourself, Then Keep Taking Clients

And this leads into the number two thing you shouldn't do when you're a virtual assistant. It's overbooking yourself, especially when it's tempting to say yes to everybody, but when a client is on the bottom of your priority list, they know it. Trust me—we're aware when you've overbooked yourself. I am a freelancer, so I know what that feels like from the freelancer perspective. But when you take on a client that you don't have the bandwidth to help, you're only hurting everybody. Limit yourself. Otherwise, you're delivering mediocre results to everybody or missing deadlines and leading to client frustration. So, know your limit. Recognize when you're feeling overwhelmed, and look at your business systems to decide what you can do better. Maybe I need to let some clients go or to bring my clients to a new minimum monthly order. But don't overbook yourself because it seems tempting to take the money. When you deliver a subpar experience, that client isn't going to want to work with you and isn't going to refer you to others.

## Fail to Ask for Further Instructions or Details

Avoid failing to ask for further instructions when you're unsure what's going on. Now, clients aren't perfect; we don't always give directions in the best way. One of the things I really like about my team members now is that if I give them material that isn't clear, they'll come back and say, "I have no idea what you're talking about. Can we get on a call quickly to figure this out" So, don't be afraid to ask for help. Nothing is embarrassing about it.

In fact, it's much better to ask for help at the beginning of the project than turning in late work or something a client didn't need because you didn't understand the directions. Always get that clarification upfront. It shows the client that you're very professional and care about the result too.

## Submit Poor Quality Work Because You Didn't Care or Ran Out of Time

Don't do something poorly or quickly, and then try to pass it off as decent work. Again, much like being overbooked, clients know when you do that. So, please don't, you know if you're supposed to be writing or editing a 2,000-word landing page, and it comes back with errors in it close to the deadline, that tells me that you didn't spend the time you were supposed to on it. It shows me that you spent about five minutes on it, particularly if you're on an hourly contract with your clients.

But what it all boils down to is be professional. Do the work you say you're going to do. When you're making a contract and a commitment to a client, hold true to that. If you've told them that you're available five hours a week, but that's inaccurate because you've overbooked yourself, that's very unfair to the client. And that means that they're getting your tired, headachy brain because you've been dealing with other clients all day long. So, give everybody the common courtesy of not overbooking you as a virtual assistant. Own up to things when you make a mistake. Don't try to pass off low-quality work as normal, and if you're unclear on the directions and need help, ask for further information.

## Not Understanding the Terms of a Non-disclosure Agreement

A non-disclosure agreement usually comes in connection with a virtual assistant contract but is typically its own document. This is because the client anticipates that you might come across information that is either proprietary to the organization or includes details that the client wishes to be kept secret. Imagine, for example, that you were helping set up the blog and social media channels for a new mobile app. If the mobile application hasn't yet launched, the client wants some peace of mind that any information you discover as part of working on that project will be kept secret and not disclosed to others. The client will likely to ask for information, such as your name and address. This information isn't out of the ordinary and is usually there to give that client a level of confidentiality and confidence that the document can be upheld legally.

Make sure you read through the terms listed in a non-disclosure agreement. Your agreement might be restrictive in the sense that you might not be able to share the work that you create for the client. This information is especially important when you're pitching other clients or showcasing work samples on your website. It's important to make sure you're not violating any of the terms inside your non-disclosure agreement when you share information such as their social media images, links on their website, or other details associated with their business. As a good rule of thumb, you should always ask the client outright whether or not you can name them as a reference or use any of the samples you create for that client in the future. Make a note of this inside your client files, so you don't ever accidentally violate a non-disclosure agreement.

# Firing Clients

When you're first getting started in your virtual assistant business, it's easy to be very excited and overlook some of the negative behavior that a potential client might express. Since you're just beginning and excited to have the money and the experience, it's easy to let this go for a while, but there are certain situations in which you need to move forward with firing your virtual assistant client.

Staying in a negative business relationship is much like staying in a toxic relationship altogether. It can do a great deal of damage to your business and your personal feelings from day to day. What follows are three clear signs that you need to terminate an existing virtual assistant client.

There are a number of reasons why you might fire a virtual assistant client.

## Refuses to Respect Your Boundaries

Suppose your client has suddenly started calling you at all hours, sending you text messages, requiring an immediate answer, or trying to get in touch with you when you told him or her you'll be on vacation. In that case, this is a sign that your virtual assistant client doesn't respect your communication boundaries. It isn't enough to simply ignore this issue as it's appropriate to bring up your concerns about this in an actual phone conversation with your client before you terminate him or her.

Your client may simply be stressed out and not realize how their behavior reflects on you. That being said, it's inappropriate and a clear sign that you need to consider terminating your client for this kind of behavior.

## They Refuse to Pay You on Time

Reasonable delays and several day turnarounds are certainly normal because not everyone processes their invoices on the same day. Still, if you're waiting for two weeks or longer for your payment to clear, you shouldn't be working during this time.

As mentioned previously, the majority of virtual assistants require payment upfront, even for ongoing contracts. This helps ensure that you're all set for the month before you begin work and helps to avoid the problem of doing a great deal of work for a client and not being paid for it. However, if a client continues to have problems with payment, especially in the situation where you are receiving it late, reach out to him or her to see if there is anything you can do to make things easier for them.

It could be that you need to adjust the day you send your invoice to the day that they pay invoices. Timing these administrative things might seem like a small issue, but it isn't a small issue when your client is likely overwhelmed with plenty of responsibilities. Remember, you're handling many projects for them that may be buried in email and other tasks. Try to make payment issues as straightforward as possible for them to handle so that you don't have stress, and they don't either.

## The Job Has Grown Outside of Its Scope

If you initially brought on a client with a flat fee or even a ten-hour per month expectation, if the job has grown but the payment hasn't, or if the stress has doubled as the job has grown, it may be time to terminate your virtual assistant client. Many clients get so excited about identifying a virtual assistant who can handle a lot of things for them that they begin to dump on this particular individual.

They expect greatness in all areas and continue to give you tasks with unreasonable deadlines. Of course, this is much like other issues with a virtual assistant client, and you should certainly bring it up with your client first before moving forward and attempting to terminate the relationship.

Remember that a lot of things can become misconstrued digitally, and it's a good idea to have phone conversations about these issues if you suspect there is a problem with your virtual assistant client.

In many cases, you can resolve communication and other issues by speaking on the phone. If you're unable to resolve these issues, you have to think carefully about whether this client is doing you more harm than good. If you're waking up every day and feeling like you're dreading going to work, what have you done besides create your day job all over again?

Many virtual assistants begin a career like this because they enjoy the freedom and flexibility it affords. Remember that part of that freedom and flexibility is in getting to choose who you work with. If you are working with someone who's no longer a fit for your current business structure, consider terminating them to make room for better opportunities.

## Consistently Poor Instructions

Instructions are the leading reason for communication breakdowns between clients and virtual assistants. Where possible, you should always provide feedback to your clients when they don't provide enough details.

One of the biggest reasons this can become a problem between a virtual assistant and a client is when the client gives unclear directions and refuses to respond or provide additional clarity. That leaves a virtual assistant responsible for coming up with answers to those key questions on their own.

Let's imagine that a client gives a virtual assistant an assignment to develop five social media posts to be shared on that client's profiles. The virtual assistant writes back and asks if there are any specific messages, graphic types, or colors included in these posts.

The client never responds despite numerous follow-ups. The virtual assistant, wanting to hold up his or her end of the bargain and complete the work, comes up with five suggested social media posts and sends them as a draft to the client. The client never responds and then sends a follow-up email wanting to know why posts were never scheduled, telling the virtual assistant to go ahead and schedule whatever was written. When the virtual assistant goes in to schedule the posts, the client then fires back shortly after the first one is published saying this isn't what I was looking for at all, please delete and take down these posts immediately.

This means that the virtual assistant is now spending more time going back and correcting things that could've been fixed much earlier in the process. When you give your clients plenty of opportunities to improve their instructions or give you additional details when it hasn't already been provided, it isn't the virtual assistant's fault when the client fails to follow through. After a couple of weeks of dealing with this, any virtual assistant would consider terminating their relationship.

If your relationship with an existing virtual assistant client has gotten to the level of true frustration, and you can no longer imagine keeping up with this responsibility, consider terminating the contract and moving on. Not every client is right for you, and it's certainly true that you may outgrow some clients throughout your business too.

## What to Do When a Client Offers You a Job You Don't Want

There may be instances that come up in your career when a client you truly enjoy working with offers to hand you a task that isn't a natural fit. While you can certainly opt to embrace the challenge of doing something new or different, there are many reasons to be totally honest about the situation.

Getting involved in a project that doesn't interest you or is outside of your defined skill set could potentially push you to the next level and open your eyes to a new way of doing business, a new project, or industry type. However, the chances that this project will be frustrating and take an abundance of time are relatively high.

Sometimes, a client will give you a project they believe is right up your alley or believe to be relatively simple. However, as freelancers, we all have specific skillsets and may prefer not to take on a particular project.

Being upfront with your client is far better than missing a deadline or turning in poor quality work. This can make the client question working with you and will only lead to confusion and potential conflict.

Being upfront is always recommended when it comes to potential issues with a client. You can say something along the lines of "thank you for the opportunity, but this isn't really in my wheelhouse. However, I know so and so who can assist with the project (or I have a team member who would be willing to work on this), but the delivery time might be a little bit longer than what you are used to as I would like to review the work before it reaches you."

This will give the client confidence that you're committed to the best possible outcome for them, even if that means that you aren't taking on the project yourself.

Suppose you're facing any one or a combination of these situations. In that case, it's important that you exercise professionalism when terminating the virtual assistant contract and identify ways to promote your business successfully. Clients who drag on your time, energy, or resources isn't recommended.

Being able to terminate the contract can allow you to bring on newer clients or explore other avenues in your business or personal life. Make sure you review the terms of the contract before you end it. You may need to give the client a certain number of days' notice, and you may want to have all of your invoices cleared up well in advance to avoid problems with payment or your business cash flow. Give them plenty of written notice so that they have time to find a replacement and ensure that any projects you're currently working on can be wrapped up effectively or handed off to another person.

# Launch Mistakes

If you spend any time in "Facebook groups" for virtual assistants, you'll hear stories of people who gave up a few weeks into pursuing their VA dream. Often, this boils down to unclear expectations or mistakes that could've been avoided. Here are some of the most common ones.

## Launch Mistake #1: Being Unclear about Your Offerings

It's one thing to be a VA who does a lot of tasks, but advertising yourself this way confuses clients. If you tell a potential client that you do pretty much everything, that'll overwhelm them. This is because as humans, we need to see a natural next step or we get frozen in inaction.

If you sense a client doesn't know where to start, ask them these questions to help target what you're offering to them:

- How much time are you spending on administrative tasks?

- What are the biggest headaches you have now in your business?

- What tasks frustrate you?

- What tasks are impossible or very difficult for you?

- How much time would you like to save?

- What's the most overwhelming aspect of your day to day?

## Launch Mistake #2: Under-charging

You're thrilled that this client might sign on the dotted line, but you realize you didn't quote enough. Now, you're stuck working for someone who might not truly value you. It's true that some of the most frustrating clients are the ones who pay the least. It seems counterintuitive, but they're often more difficult to work with and expect a lot more out of you.

You need to charge a living wage. Finding this out can be a bit of trial and error, but most virtual assistants charge by the hour or by the flat package rate for various services.

Do your homework! If you're just starting out, you can learn a lot by taking a peek at the competition. This gives you good insight into what is reasonable in the marketplace. Typically, the more comprehensive the task, the higher the hourly rate.

When you charge too little, you're very likely to get burned out and will want to give up. This isn't a positive experience for you or your clients, so avoid it altogether by putting together a compelling offering and a wage that pays you what you're worth.

## Launch Mistake #3: Launching to Crickets

There's a lot of hype out there that you need a website, a hosting plan, a bustling blog, profiles on major job board sites, and more before you get started. What you need is a targeted action plan, so don't get hung up on spending a lot of time or money on a website. If you put together a site and no one visits it, this can be soul-crushing.

Here's where I repeat one of those mantras that comes up again and again when I work with potential VAs: The most important thing you can do as a new VA is to enroll clients.

If you can set up a simple website in an hour or so using a tool like Wix or Squarespace, then do it. But don't assume that people will visit a website just because you built it.

Remember, you're not making money unless you're booking clients. Sales calls and contacting clients is the most important thing you can do when you start a VA business. Don't allow yourself to fall victim to distraction; you can't afford it! Right now, make your goal to be enrolling clients and finding new people to work with on job boards, groups, and direct outreach.

You can even use games to reward yourself. If you can't design a site or you need cash flow for some other purpose (like a new computer to support your VA biz), set a booking goal. After you've booked five clients, allow yourself to make that purchase of the web designer or the new computer. Get those clients enrolled and paid first, though!

Making a game of it is a great strategy for pushing yourself and staying out of inaction mode. You have something on the line that you want for doing the hard part (booking clients). Once you start putting yourself out there, it's much easier to keep your momentum going as you enroll clients.

## Launch Mistake #4: Hiring the Wrong Clients

Every person that needs a VA isn't the right one for you. If you're going to get involved in a long-term relationship, would you commit the next year of your life based on a blind date? Most likely not. The same goes for VA clients. This has to be someone you can interact with regularly, so make sure you're bringing on your ideal clients and not those who push your boundaries or pay too little.

If you already have a nightmare client, find a way out of it. Use games to push yourself to book someone new (or even better, two new clients!) and then, get out of the bad relationship. You shouldn't have to stay committed to a situation that isn't working for you anymore.

What's the number one thing you're nervous about with your new VA business? If you're launching soon, what are you most nervous about? Chime in by visiting my "Facebook group," which you can find at bit.ly/upworkgroup.

# Conclusion: What's Next for You?

Now you know all of the most important steps for launching a virtual assistant business. But it's easy to still feel like you have a long way to go. There are a lot of things to consider in launching your VA business. That's why I've made it super easy for you to get started with all the necessary templates in a workbook that's available on www.virtualassistantbook.com. You can also get more details about how to purchase a coaching session to get feedback before you launch! I'm honored to have been part of your journey and I can't wait to see what you accomplish.

Before you go, now that you made it this far, can you do me a big favor? Whether you've followed my journey into book publishing or not, you probably already realize just how important reviews are! In fact, you might have purchased this book because of someone else's review. I want to know what you think, and other readers do, too. If you could spend a few minutes writing what you thought of this book on Amazon or Goodreads, it would mean the world to me. I wrote this book because there are lots of great courses out there- but many of them are geared towards beginner virtual assistants and are priced in the hundreds of dollars. I wanted to create something affordable and accessible for everyone so that you can get your business started today. Thanks for being a reader! Cheers to your VA business. Now get to work!

# ABOUT THE AUTHOR

Laura Briggs is empowering the freelance generation. Through her public speaking, coaching, and writing, she helps freelancers build the business of their dreams without sacrificing all their time, family, or sanity. Laura burned out as an inner city middle school teacher before become an accidental freelancer with a Google search for "how to become a freelance writer." Since then, she's become a contributor for Entrepreneur and Business Insider and has been featured as a guest expert on over 150 podcasts. She worked with more than 300 clients around the world, including Microsoft, TrueCar, and the Mobile Marketing Association. Laura has delivered two TEDx talks on the power of the freelance economy for enabling freedom and flexibility and how it's being used to address the technical skills gap in the U.S. She's also the founder of Operation Freelance, a national 501(c)3 that provides free 90-day training and certifications in freelancing to military spouses and veterans.

CPSIA information can be obtained
at www.ICGtesting.com
Printed in the USA
LVHW030519120422
715973LV00015B/97